11.01

EXPRESS REVIEW GUIDES

D1613698

Reading Comprehension

Reading Comprehension

New York

Library of Congress Cataloging-in-Publication Data:
Express review guides. Reading comprehension.
  p. cm.
 ISBN: 978-1-57685-622-2
1. Reading comprehension. I. LearningExpress (Organization).
 LB1050.45.E97 2008
 428.4076—dc22

2008000921

Printed in the United States of America

9 8 7 6 5 4 3 2 1

First Edition

ISBN: 978-1-57685-622-2

For more information or to place an order, contact LearningExpress at:
    55 Broadway
    8th Floor
    New York, NY 10006

Or visit us at:
    www.learnatest.com

Contents

INTRODUCTION   v

PRETEST   ix

CHAPTER 1   Getting the Essential Information   1

CHAPTER 2   Finding the Main Idea   15

CHAPTER 3   Fact versus Opinion   27

CHAPTER 4   Chronological Order   37

CHAPTER 5   Order of Importance   49

CHAPTER 6   Compare and Contrast   59

CHAPTER 7   Point of View   71

CHAPTER 8   Style, Diction, and Tone   85

CHAPTER 9   Emotional versus Logical Appeal   97

CHAPTER 10   Meaning in Literature   105

POSTTEST   115

GLOSSARY   129

Introduction

Imagine not being able to read. Of course, you wouldn't be reading this, let alone all the other things you read every day without even really noticing! Think about it. Think about all the words you read on any given day. You might read restaurant menus, homework instructions, street signs, newspaper headlines, or somebody's T-shirt. You might read magazines and books for school, or just for fun. If you didn't know how to read, imagine how frustrated you'd feel. It'd be as if the whole world was in on some inside joke and you just didn't get it!

Well, you've read this far, so clearly you can read. Phew, good thing! But are you getting the most out of it? Reading comprehension is just that—comprehending, or understanding, what you read. It's all well and good if you can read a newspaper article, but do you *really* understand what you're reading? If you don't, or even if you do, this book is for you. It's about getting the most out of what you read, so you don't read something just to say you read it. You read it, and you really get it. You understand what the writer is saying and the arguments he or she is trying to make. Having the *ability* to read is an essential skill, but what's the point if you don't understand what you're reading?

HOW TO USE THIS BOOK

This book will show you how to become an active reader—someone who not only reads, but connects with what's written. The main goal is to be involved with what you read and to think about what the writer's really trying to communicate to you. This book also includes the following helpful hints and exercises to help you further develop your writing skills:

➡ *Fuel for Thought*: critical information and definitions that can help you learn more about a particular topic

➡ *Inside Track*: tips for reducing your study and practice time—without sacrificing accuracy

➡ *Caution!*: pitfalls to be on the lookout for

➡ *Pace Yourself*: extra activities for added practice

➡ *Practice Lap*: quick practice exercises and activities to let you test your knowledge

Each chapter in this book has a lesson, some practice questions, and a short recap. At the end of each chapter are the answers to the practice questions. Here's a sneak peek at what the chapters hold in store:

CHAPTER 1: GETTING THE ESSENTIAL INFORMATION

Here you find strategies to help you get all the essential information from what you read.

CHAPTER 2: FINDING THE MAIN IDEA

What is a main idea and how do you identify it? That's what this lesson will show you.

CHAPTER 3: FACT VERSUS OPINION

Some things are true and some things aren't. This chapter helps you figure out the difference and explains why it's important to know the difference. And that's a fact!

CHAPTER 4: CHRONOLOGICAL ORDER

Everything in life happens in chronological order. But what exactly does that mean . . . and how do you identify it in text?

CHAPTER 5: ORDER OF IMPORTANCE

Some things are more important than others, so sometimes writers structure their text in the order of importance. This chapter shows you how to recognize the structure to get more out of what you read.

CHAPTER 6: COMPARE AND CONTRAST

Sometimes authors use similarities and differences between things to express their ideas. You'll discover how to recognize this strategy and how to distinguish whether something is being compared or contrasted.

CHAPTER 7: POINT OF VIEW

There are three different points of view, or perspectives, from which a story can be told. In this chapter, you'll discover what the three points of view are and how to identify which is being used!

CHAPTER 8: STYLE, DICTION, AND TONE

What are style, diction, and tone? How are these more subtle aspects of writing used and how can you identify them in text? Check out this chapter to find out.

CHAPTER 9: EMOTIONAL VERSUS LOGICAL APPEAL

Sometimes in writing, you're faced with an argument. The author may use logical appeal or emotional appeal to persuade you to agree with his or her argument. What's the difference, and why does it matter? Find out in this chapter.

CHAPTER 10: MEANING IN LITERATURE

This chapter demystifies the task of finding a theme in literature.

And that's not all! There's a pretest you'll find right before Chapter 1. Take the test before you start the first lesson. Don't worry about how much you know or how many questions you get right or wrong; you're not supposed to be good at this yet! After Chapter 10, there's a posttest. Don't worry about this one either; by the time you've worked your way through this book, you'll ace it! At the very end is a glossary that contains an extensive list of important words you may already know, or you may learn throughout this book. Refer to it as often as you need to.

Pretest

The following pretest contains 50 questions and is designed to test your knowledge of various topics that will be covered in the book. By taking this test and checking your answers against the answer key that follows, you'll discover what you already know and what you need to learn. For each question you answer incorrectly, be sure to read the explanation that accompanies the correct answer in the answer key. Also, the answer key contains chapter references, so that you know which lesson deals with that question's topic. It should take you no more than two hours to complete the pretest. Good luck!

Read the passage and answer questions 1–4.

> Next Saturday, October 14, there will be a concert in Jefferson Park to benefit the Jefferson County Parks and Recreation Department. The concert will begin at 7:00 P.M. and will include such acts as the community jazz band and the local choir. Tickets are five dollars and are available at the park's information booth. All proceeds will go to the Parks and Recreation Department and will be used to maintain the beauty of all our local parks.

1. Where is the concert?

2. When is the concert?

3. How much are tickets?

4. What do the ticket sales benefit?

Identify whether each of the following is a *subject* or a *main idea*.

5. mushroom barley soup

6. dangerous aspects of archery

7. board games

8. patchwork quilts

9. benefits of bicycling

Read the passage and answer questions 10 and 11.

> Robert received a scholarship to attend a local college. The scholarship enabled Robert to buy books for his classes, which is something that can end up costing a lot of money. Without the scholarship, Robert might not have been able to afford the books that he needed for his classes. Robert's scholarship also created a situation in which Robert did not have to get a part-time job while attending school. This gave Robert more time to study, and he was able to excel in his courses.

10. How did Robert's scholarship affect his studies?

11. What is the main idea of this passage?

12. A topic sentence is always
    a. the first sentence in a paragraph.
    b. a general idea.
    c. regarding a controversial topic.
    d. the last sentence in a paragraph.

Identify whether each of the following statements is a *fact* or an *opinion*.

13. Music makes exercising more enjoyable.

14. I painted my walls my favorite shade of blue.

15. It's better to buy in bulk when you can.

16. Some windows can be drafty in the winter.

17. Swimming in the ocean is relaxing.

18. Rewrite the following paragraph so that it is in chronological order.

But when I got to the front door with the bag of garbage in my hand, I couldn't find my shoes. I got up to answer it, but it was a wrong number. Then, because I was already awake, I decided to go downstairs and put the garbage out by the curb. After searching the bottom of the closet, I finally found my shoes and was able to go outside. I was still sleeping this morning when the telephone rang.

Identify the *cause* and *effect* in each of the following statements.

19. It was so cold out that I had to wear a hat.

20. The traffic jam caused Mary to be late for school.

21. John couldn't reach the paper on the top shelf because it was too high.

22. The effect of leaving the ice cream out on the counter is that it melts.

23. Turning the lights off during the day will save energy.

Read the passage and answer questions 24 and 25.

If you are lucky enough to have a yard or access to a public park, then perhaps you have had the opportunity to do some gardening. Many people use the space in their yards or public parks to plant various types of trees, bushes, and flowers. There are many reasons why these people find gardening to be such a rewarding and enjoyable hobby.

Most importantly, gardening can be a way of meditating. It is often time that a person can use to ponder his or her thoughts and feelings. This time can be used to really relax and release some of the stress that is part of a person's daily life. The alone time, combined with the outdoor setting and the methodical nature of gardening itself, offers a meditative state of relaxation.

The act of gardening not only releases stress, but it also beautifies the Earth. Whether it's in someone's yard or a public park, adding flowers and trees to the area makes a much more pleasant environment in which to stroll, play, or just sit with a good book.

Lastly, while not as important as its meditative nature or its act of beautification, gardening can also be enjoyable for what it can give a person in return. If a person plants fruits and vegetables, he or she can then harvest them and use them to cook meals. If someone plants flowers, he or she can cut them and bring them inside to liven up the home. A person can even plant certain types of plants that attract various species of butterflies and birds so that he or she can watch the animals fly through the garden.

These are all reasons why people garden and why they enjoy the popular hobby. If you haven't already, maybe someday you'll have the opportunity to plant trees and flowers and maybe you'll find the activity just as rewarding.

24. List the reasons given for why gardening is enjoyable in the order that they appear in the passage.

25. What do you notice about the order in which the reasons appear?

Read the passage and answer questions 26 and 27.

In many ways, living in an apartment building is like living in a tree house. If you live on any other floor but the ground floor of an apartment building, you might have to go upstairs to get to your front door. A tree house would also require you to climb up some sort of stairs to get home. Also, in an apartment building, you could be higher than other buildings around you, much like you would be if your tree house was built on a high branch. In both an apartment and a tree house, it is quite possible that you could look out of your window at the tops of trees and feel like you were right there among them.

26. Are apartments and tree houses being compared or contrasted in the passage?

27. What three aspects of apartment living and tree house living are mentioned?

For questions 28–32, identify whether the *first-*, *second-*, or *third-person point of view* is being used in each sentence.

28. You need a ticket to get into the concert.

29. She did a backflip off the diving board and everyone cheered.

30. Paul likes to sit in the back row of the movie theater.

31. I can smell the cake baking all throughout the house.

32. My shoelaces are untied.

Identify whether the sentences in questions 33–37 are *objective* or *subjective*.

33. We had a lot of fun playing tag in the park the other day.

34. House plants release oxygen into the air.

35. Sunday is the first day of the week.

36. It is difficult to wake up on Monday mornings.

37. There are some pizzerias that make rectangular pizzas instead of round ones.

38. What is the connotation of the underlined word in the following sentence?
I am so tired of the <u>drudgeries</u> that my job requires of me.
 a. that the author is looking for a new job
 b. that the author needs more sleep
 c. that the author feels that he or she is worthy of a better job
 d. that this is the first job about which the author has had an opinion

Using the list below, identify the tone of following sentences in questions 39–42.
 hopeful
 sincere
 threatening
 excited

39. Don't you dare talk to me like that!

40. I really wish I had been there.

41. The soccer team made the state finals!

42. Maybe tomorrow the sun will come out.

For questions 43–47, identify whether each appeal is *logical* or *emotional*.

43. You wouldn't want to put off paying your electric bill, because you'd end up feeling badly about it later.

44. Studies have shown that some chocolate has health benefits.

45. Recent polls suggest that healthcare is an important issue with voters.

46. If you don't look both ways before you cross the street, you risk being hit by a car.

47. The new fountain in the center of the park will really add a nice ambiance.

Read Robert Frost's poem "The Road Not Taken" and answer questions 48–50.

> Two roads diverged in a yellow wood,
> And sorry I could not travel both
> And be one traveler, long I stood
> And looked down one as far as I could
> To where it bent in the undergrowth;
>
> Then took the other, as just as fair
> And having perhaps the better claim,
> Because it was grassy and wanted wear;
> Though as for that, the passing there
> Had worn them really about the same,
>
> And both that morning equally lay
> In leaves no step had trodden black
> Oh, I kept the first for another day!
> Yet knowing how way leads on to way,
> I doubted if I should ever come back.
>
> I shall be telling this with a sigh
> Somewhere ages and ages hence:
> Two roads diverged in a wood, and I—
> I took the one less traveled by,
> And that has made all the difference.

48. What is the action of the poem?

49. What is the tone of the poem?

50. What is the theme of the poem?

ANSWERS

The answers to questions 1 through 4 can all be found in the passage and are very straightforward. When you first read the passage, you should've circled, underlined, or made notes about the essential information. (For more information on this concept, see Chapter 1.)

Here is an example of what your notes for questions 1 through 4 might look like:

> Next Saturday, October 14, there will be a concert in Jefferson Park to benefit the Jefferson County Parks and Recreation Department. The concert will begin at 7:00 P.M. and will include such acts as the community jazz band and the local choir. Tickets are five dollars and are available at the park's information booth. All proceeds will go to the Parks and Recreation department and will be used to maintain the beauty of all our local parks.

1. The concert is in Jefferson Park.
2. The concert is next Saturday, October 14.
3. Tickets are five dollars.
4. Ticket sales benefit the Parks and Recreation Department.
5. subject

   A passage could be *about* mushroom barley soup, but what is being *said about* the soup would be a main idea. So, *mushroom barley soup* is a subject, but not a main idea. (For more information on this concept, see Chapter 2.)
6. main idea

   Dangerous aspects of archery is an idea that needs more support. What are the aspects? Why are they dangerous? This general idea needs support, so it is a main idea. (For more information on this concept, see Chapter 2.)
7. subject

   This is a subject because it is a specific thing that doesn't need support. Something would need to be said *about* board games in order for it to be a main idea. (For more information on this concept, see Chapter 2.)
8. subject

Patchwork quilts is a subject because it is not an idea that needs support. (For more information on this concept, see Chapter 2.)

9. main idea

This is a main idea because it needs support to back it up. What are the benefits of bicycling? How are they beneficial? (For more information on this concept, see Chapter 2.)

10. Robert's scholarship gave him more time to study, and because he didn't need to get a job, it allowed him to buy books with which to do that studying. The answer to this question can be found directly in the passage. After carefully reading the passage, you find that Robert used his scholarship money to buy books for school. The money enabled him to spend his time studying instead of working at a job. (For more information on this concept, see Chapter 2.)

11. The main idea is that scholarships can be very helpful to students who need them. Because the main idea of the passage is not explicitly stated, you need to use your powers of observation to discover what it is. Start with what you know. You know that Robert received a scholarship and you know that it helped him in at least two ways that are discussed in the passage. What idea does this information seem to support? It seems to support the idea that scholarships can be very helpful to those who need them. (For more information on this concept, see Chapter 2.)

12. **b.** A topic sentence is always a general idea. Although choice **a** states that it may be the first sentence of a paragraph, it doesn't have to be. It also doesn't have to be based on a controversial topic as stated in choice **c**, and usually, it is not the last sentence of a paragraph as stated in choice **d.** (For more information on this concept, see Chapter 2.)

13. opinion

It's possible that not everyone thinks music makes exercising more enjoyable. Because of this, it is an opinion. (For more information on this concept, see Chapter 3.)

14. fact

Although I might have an opinion about a certain shade of blue, I chose that color to paint my wall; it is something that actually occurred, and therefore, it is a fact. (For more information on this concept, see Chapter 3.)

15. opinion

It's debatable whether buying in bulk is better than not buying in bulk. That makes this an opinion. (For more information on this concept, see Chapter 3.)

16. fact

    It can't be debated that some windows can be drafty in the winter. There are definitely windows out there in the world that are drafty. Because this cannot be debated, it is a fact. (For more information on this concept, see Chapter 3.)

17. opinion

    Some people might not agree that swimming in the ocean is relaxing. This is an opinion, not a fact. (For more information on this concept, see Chapter 3.)

18. *I was still sleeping this morning when the telephone rang. I got up to answer it, but it was a wrong number. Then, because I was already awake, I decided to go downstairs and put the garbage out by the curb. But when I got to the front door with the bag of garbage in my hand, I couldn't find my shoes. After searching the bottom of the closet, I finally found my shoes and was able to go outside.*

    Because you know that the person was still sleeping when the phone rang, everything else must have happened after that. A person usually answers the phone after hearing it ring, so that comes next. You can tell the decision to take out the trash comes next because of the phrase, *Then, because I was already awake.* . . . After this, you discover the person must not have been able to find his or her shoes before he or she *finally found* them. (For more information on this concept, see Chapter 4.)

19. cause = the cold temperature

    effect = I had to wear a hat

    The cold temperature was the cause of my having to wear a hat, and my wearing a hat was the effect of the cold temperature. (For more information on this concept, see Chapter 4.)

20. cause = traffic jam

    effect = Mary was late to school

    The traffic jam was the cause of Mary being late to school, and Mary being late to school was the effect of the traffic jam. (For more information on this concept, see Chapter 4.)

21. cause = the shelf was too high

    effect = John couldn't reach the shelf

The shelf's height was the cause of John not being able to reach it, and John not being able to reach the shelf was the effect of it being too high. (For more information on this concept, see Chapter 4.)

22. cause = ice cream left on the counter

    effect = the ice cream melts

    Ice cream left out on the counter is the cause of it melting, and the ice cream melting is the effect of leaving out on the counter. (For more information on this concept, see Chapter 4.)

23. cause = turning off the lights during the day

    effect = save energy

    Turning off the lights during the day causes a saving of energy, and the saving of energy is the effect of turning off the lights during the day. (For more information on this concept, see Chapter 4.)

Here is the passage that pertains to questions 24 and 25 with the relevant information underlined.

If you are lucky enough to have a yard or access to a public park, then perhaps you have had the opportunity to do some gardening. Many people use the space in their yards or public parks to plant various types of trees, bushes, and flowers. There are many reasons why these people find gardening to be such a rewarding and enjoyable hobby.

Most importantly, gardening can be a way of meditating. It is often time that a person can use to ponder his or her thoughts and feelings. This time can be used to really relax and release some of the stress that is part of a person's daily life. The alone time, combined with the outdoor setting and the methodical nature of gardening itself, offers a meditative state of relaxation.

The act of gardening not only releases stress, but it also beautifies the Earth. Whether it's in someone's own yard or a public park, adding flowers and trees to the area makes a much more pleasant environment in which to stroll, play, or just sit with a good book.

Lastly, while not as important as its meditative nature or its act of beautification, gardening can also be enjoyable for what it can give a person in return. If a person plants fruits and vegetables, he or she can then harvest them and use them to cook meals. If a person plants flowers, he or she can cut them and bring them inside to liven up his or her home. A person can even plant certain types of plants that attract various species of butterflies and birds, so that he or she can watch the animals fly through his or her garden.

These are all reasons why people garden and why they enjoy the popular hobby. If you haven't already, maybe someday you'll have the opportunity to plant trees and flowers and maybe you'll find the activity just as rewarding.

24. The reasons given for why gardening is enjoyable is that gardening is meditative, gardening beautifies the Earth, and gardening can give back to a person.

As you were reading, you should have noticed the reasons gardening is enjoyable. Their order of appearance is clear once you know what the reasons are. Also, notice how each reason is the topic sentence of its paragraph. (For more information on this concept, see Chapter 5.)

25. The reasons gardening is enjoyable are listed in order of importance, starting with the most important and ending with the least important. You know that the first reason is the most important because the sentence begins with *Most importantly*. . . . Similarly, you know that the last reason is the least important, because the author states that it is not as important as the first two reasons. (For more information on this concept, see Chapter 5.)

Here is the passage that pertains to questions 26 and 27 with the relevant information underlined.

In many ways, living in an apartment building is <u>like</u> living in a tree house. If you live on any other floor but the ground floor of an apartment building, you might <u>have to go upstairs</u> to get to your front door. A tree house would <u>also</u> require you to climb up some sort of stairs to get home. <u>Also</u> in an apartment building, you could be <u>higher than other buildings around you</u>, much <u>like</u> you would be if your tree house was built on a high branch. In <u>both</u> an apartment and a tree house, it is quite possible that you could <u>look out of your window at the tops of trees</u> and feel like you were right there among them.

26. Apartments and tree houses are being compared.

    There are some clue words you should've noticed in the passage that would have demonstrated why apartments and tree houses were being compared and not contrasted. Those words are *like*, *also*, and *both*. (For more information on this concept, see Chapter 6.)

27. The three aspects mentioned are climbing up stairs, being high up, and looking out your window at the tops of trees.

    As you read, you might've made notes or circled things you thought were important within the passage. When things are compared or contrasted, aspects of both things are discussed. These aspects are important to observe because they are a large part of understanding the comparison. (For more information on this concept, see Chapter 6.)

28. second person

    The sentence refers to *you*, so this is the second-person point of view. (For more information on this concept, see Chapter 7.)

29. third person

    This is the third-person point of view, because the author is not involved. The sentence refers to a *she*. (For more information on this concept, see Chapter 7.)

30. third person

    Paul is the subject of this sentence, so this is the third-person point of view. (For more information on this concept, see Chapter 7.)

31. first person

    This sentence expresses an experience of the author, who identifies himself or herself as *I*. Therefore, it is written in the first-person point of view. (For more information on this concept, see Chapter 7.)

32. first person

    The speaker of this sentence uses the word *my*, which tells you that it is written in the first-person point of view. (For more information on this concept, see Chapter 7.)

33. subjective

    Because this sentence expresses the author's experience, it is subjective and not objective. (For more information on this concept, see Chapter 7.)

34. objective

The fact that house plants release oxygen into the air does not directly relate to the author's experience, so it is objective. (For more information on this concept, see Chapter 7.)

35. objective

It is a well-known, objective fact that Sunday is the first day of the week. (For more information on this concept, see Chapter 7.)

36. subjective

The author of this sentence finds it difficult to wake up on Monday mornings, but the experience is not necessarily universal. It is subjective because it expresses the experience of the author. (For more information on this concept, see Chapter 7.)

37. objective

It is an objective statement, or a statement of fact, to say that some pizzerias make rectangular pizzas instead of round ones. Although the author may have experienced this herself or himself, it is expressed as an objective statement. (For more information on this concept, see Chapter 7.)

38. c. The connotation of *drudgery* is work that's menial or basic. So used in this sentence, the word indicates that the author finds the job to be beneath his or her abilities. (For more information on this concept, see Chapter 8.)

39. threatening

The content of this sentence is clearly a threat, because the reader is being told very sternly not to talk to the author like that. (For more information on this concept, see Chapter 8.)

40. sincere

The author uses *really* to emphasis sincerity. (For more information on this concept, see Chapter 8.)

41. excited

The exclamation point indicates passion or excitement. (For more information on this concept, see Chapter 8.)

42. hopeful

The *maybe* at the beginning of this sentence sets a hopeful tone. (For more information on this concept, see Chapter 8.)

43. emotional

People don't want to feel bad about things. This argument appeals to that emotional sentiment. (For more information on this concept, see Chapter 8.)

44. logical

This argument is logical because it points to an actual study about chocolate and its health benefits. It appeals to the reader's sense of reason. (For more information on this concept, see Chapter 9.)

45. logical

This argument also appeals to reason and is therefore a logical appeal. (For more information on this concept, see Chapter 9.)

46. emotional

Nobody wants to get hit by a car! But this argument makes no attempt to reason that fewer people get hit when they look both ways. The appeal is directed towards the reader's emotions. (For more information on this concept, see Chapter 9.)

47. emotional

There is no evidence to back the argument that the fountain will add a nice ambiance. This argument appeals solely to the reader's emotions regarding a nice ambiance in the park. (For more information on this concept, see Chapter 9.)

Here is Robert Frost's poem "The Road Not Taken" that pertains to questions 48 through 50. Some words and phrases have been underlined to help explain the answers.

Two roads diverged in a yellow wood,
And sorry I could not travel both
And be one traveler, long I stood
And looked down one as far as I could
To where it bent in the undergrowth;

Then took the other, as just as fair
And having perhaps the better claim,
Because it was grassy and wanted wear;
Though as for that, the passing there
Had worn them really about the same,

<u>And both that morning equally lay</u>
In leaves no step had trodden black
Oh, I kept the first for another day!
Yet knowing how way leads on to way,
I doubted if I should ever come back.

<u>I shall be telling this with a sigh</u>
Somewhere ages and ages hence:
Two roads diverged in a wood, and I—
<u>I took the one less traveled by,</u>
<u>And that has made all the difference.</u>

48. The action of the poem is based on the speaker's travels. The speaker is traveling, comes to a fork, and looks down each path. He decides to take the one that looks slightly less traveled. He figures he can save the other path for another day, but realizes he probably won't be back this way again. Years later, when he tells the story, he knows he made the right choice by taking the path less traveled. (For more information on this concept, see Chapter 10.)

49. Because this poem is a story that is being told to you, the tone is very matter-of-fact and indifferent. The speaker is essentially saying, "This is what happened." At the end, the first line of the last stanza changes the tone a bit by mentioning that he would tell the story with a *sigh*. However, up until this point in the poem, there is no indication of specific feelings the speaker might have relating to his decision; he just sort of walks you through his thought process. The sigh at the end is an indication that he's given the story some thought. (For more information on this concept, see Chapter 10.)

50. The theme of any poem relies on its action and tone. As action varies, tone may vary. The action at the beginning of this poem is the act of making a decision: which path to travel. The first portion of the poem has an indifferent, matter-of-fact tone because Frost is relaying that at the time, it didn't seem to matter very much which path the narrator chose. There is no way for the narrator to know in advance how the decision will affect him in the future. At one point, he even thought he might have a chance to go back and take the other path. Therefore, the tone is matter-of-fact as the poem reports the actions of making a decision for which there is no known outcome.

At the end of the poem, Frost talks about the narrator telling the story with a *sigh* once he realizes he chose the correct path. Here, the tone is more thoughtful and indicates that he's thought more about the decision since making it. He thinks he's made the right decision. But how can he know? The only reason he would conclude he'd taken the correct path is that he's happy about where it led him, and that seems to be the case at the end of this poem. The theme of the poem is that while we don't always know the outcome of our decisions when we make them, we can always look back and see how the decisions we made affected where we are now. (For more information on this concept, see Chapter 10.)

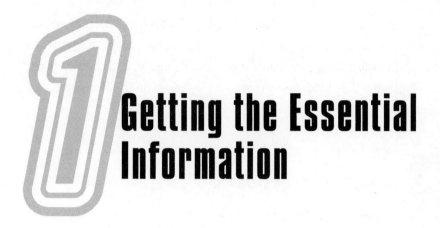

Getting the Essential Information

Have you ever read something and then, almost as soon as you put it down, forget what it was you read? We've all done that. Many times we're just in such a hurry and we don't take time to really pay attention to the details of what we're reading. Think about everything you've read today. Can you remember it all? Probably not. A lot of what we read isn't meant to be remembered for any significant length of time. For instance, think of a restaurant menu. When you read it, you need to remember what you read so you know what to order. But aside from that, it's probably not important to remember *all* the stuff you read! However, sometimes it's very important to remember what you read, and a lot of what you read for school falls into this category. Your teacher assigns you something to read with the intention that you'll learn from it—not just read it and move on. When you want to actually learn something from a text, you don't just read it, you *comprehend* it. That's what this book is all about.

PACE YOURSELF

SPEND A WHOLE day noticing what you read. Keep a notebook with you and record every time you read something. At the end of the day, look at your notes. You'll be surprised at how much you've read!

In reading comprehension, it's important to be an **active reader**. That's someone who focuses on what he or she is reading and connects with it. So instead of reading like they would a restaurant menu, active readers really *learn* from what they read. If you're wondering how you can become an active reader, read on!

FUEL FOR THOUGHT

THE OPPOSITE OF active is passive. *Passive* means lacking in energy or will.

FUEL FOR THOUGHT

IF YOU READ every word in this book, you'll have read more than 32,000 words!

The first step in becoming an active reader is to get in there and dissect the text. No, don't rip up the page or anything like that! This just means that you want to read each sentence slowly and carefully, and extract every little bit of information that you can from it. If you're thinking that it'll take a long time to focus so intently on each sentence, you're right—but it's worth the time. When you first start it may take a long time, but as you learn what to look for, you'll know exactly what to extract—and fast!

PACE YOURSELF

ACTIVE READING OFTEN requires going back and rereading something to get more information. Count the number of times the word *the* appears in the previous paragraph.

Every day you come across text that contains valuable information, and every day you dissect text without even thinking about it. Whether it's a travel guide, a recipe, or instructions for how to play a game, you naturally break down what you're reading to get the information you need. With a recipe for example, you ask yourself questions: "What ingredients do I need?" "How long do I bake it?" "When do I put in the eggs?" For a travel guide, you might ask other questions: "When do I go?" "What should I see?" "How do I use the transportation system once I get there?"

PACE YOURSELF

THINK OF THREE other things you read every day in order to get information.

You'll notice that the questions you ask have something in common. They all use one of the question words. You probably know them already, but here's a quick review:

who
what
when
where
why
how

When you're an active reader, you look for answers to certain questions: What happened? Who was involved? When did it happen? The answers to such questions give you the basic facts in the text you're reading. Getting those basic facts is the first step on the way to reading comprehension.

FIND A NEWSPAPER article and see if you can extract the basic information by asking who, what, when, where, why, and how.

The following passage is similar to an article that you might find in a newspaper. Read it to find the basic information. First, read it carefully, marking anything you think is important or that you have a question about.

> On Friday, October 21, at approximately 8:30 A.M., Judith Reynolds, owner of The Cupcake Factory, arrived at her establishment to find that it had been robbed and vandalized overnight. The front window of the shop at 128 Broad Street was broken, and chairs and tables were overturned throughout the café area. Additionally, the cash register had been pried open and emptied of money. The thieves attempted to open the safe as well, but were unsuccessful. Ms. Reynolds used her cell phone to report the crime to the police. She also phoned the proprietor of Primo Pizza, located at 130 Broad Street, as she noticed that the door of that restaurant showed signs of forced entry. The police department is asking anyone with information to call 555-2323.

Now think about the following questions:

> What happened?
> When was the crime discovered?
> Who discovered the crime?
> Where did the crime occur?

The answers to these questions give you the basic information you need to really understand what the passage is about. Here are the answers:

> What happened?
> The Cupcake Factory was robbed and vandalized.

When was the crime discovered?
Friday, October 2, at 8:30 A.M.

Who discovered the crime?
Judith Reynolds, owner of The Cupcake Factory

Who called the police?
Judith Reynolds

Where did the crime occur?
at The Cupcake Factory, which is located at 128 Broad Street

Sometimes reading might seem overwhelming because you're given so much information all at once. So, break the information down into more manageable pieces! It's sort of like eating. You don't sit down to breakfast and stuff a whole pancake in your mouth. (Well, we hope you don't, anyway!) Your mouth would be too full even to chew, so you cut the pancake into smaller pieces so it's easier to eat. Well, breaking down information in text is just as simple. Just ask yourself one question at a time, and don't try to understand everything right away. Even if you have to go back and reread to find an answer, just take it one question at a time.

INSIDE TRACK

DON'T HESITATE TO mark up the text in this book as you read. Circle, underline, or highlight anything you think is important. Make notes in the margin, or use sticky notes!

Of course, not all the questions you ask yourself will be the exactly like the ones about The Cupcake Factory robbery, but they'll be the same kinds of questions. Suppose you read a passage about ice cream. You might ask:

Who makes ice cream?
How is ice cream made?
Where do they make it?

When do people eat ice cream?

What is the most popular ice cream flavor?

Why are we even talking about ice cream?

That last question is tricky. Think about the robbery again. If you asked your-self why the robbery occurred that particular night, you might have a hard time finding the answer. But there are other *why* questions you could answer, like why Ms. Reynolds called the police (because her store had been robbed). When it comes to why some things happen, we can't always be sure, and spec-ulation is not fact. So you may not be able to answer some questions, but that's okay!

Even if you can't answer a question, however, it's still important to ask it. Let's go back to that hypothetical ice cream passage. Pretend you've read a passage about ice cream. It's helpful to ask yourself the last question we sug-gested, "Why are we even talking about ice cream?" It's important to ask that question because, even if we don't know the answer, it'll help us think about why someone wrote the passage in the first place! What was the author's pur-pose? Is it purely educational, to inform readers, or does the author have a different agenda? That aspect of reading comprehension is covered in Chapter 2, but for now, keep those questions in mind!

Take a look at another passage and see if you can dissect it to get the essen-tial information. Read the passage, and then we'll take it step by step.

The town of Wakeville is looking forward to rooting for their Wakeville Wildcats in the big football game on Friday night. If the Wildcats win the game, they will qualify for the state finals. So far this season, the Wildcats have won eight out of ten of their games, but this Friday, they face their toughest opponent yet. They will play the Tollytown Tigers, who are undefeated this season. The big game will start at 8:00 P.M. and will be played at Wakeville High School's John Reed Field.

Now that you've read the passage, here are some questions:

Who is playing in the game?

What happens if the Wildcats win?

Where will the game take place?

When is the game?

Why are the Tigers tough opponents?

The next step is to reread the passage and find the answers to our questions. As you reread, underline, circle, or highlight anything you think is important.

> The town of Wakeville is looking forward to rooting for their Wakeville Wildcats in the big football game on <u>Friday night</u>. <u>If the Wildcats win the game, they will qualify for the state finals</u>. So far this season, the Wildcats have won eight out of ten of their games, but this Friday, they face their toughest opponent yet. They will play the <u>Tollytown Tigers, who are undefeated this season</u>. <u>The big game will start at 8:00 P.M.</u> and <u>will be played at Wakeville High School's John Reed Field.</u>

Here are the questions again, along with the answers that we found in the passage:

Who is playing in the game?

the Wakeville Wildcats and the Tollytown Tigers

What happens if the Wildcats win?

They will qualify for the state finals.

Where will the game take place?

Wakeville High School's John Reed Field

When is the game?

8:00 P.M. Friday

Why are the Tigers tough opponents?

They are undefeated this season.

See how easy that was? All the information is right there in the passage. All you have to do is dig in and find it.

CAUTION!

IF YOU READ too fast, you might miss something, so be sure to go slowly. However, if you don't remember something that you read the first time, don't worry. Just read it again more carefully.

Let's try another one together. The following passage is a recipe for chocolate chip cookies. Read through it once and then we'll ask ourselves some questions to get the basic information.

Chocolate Chip Cookies

You will need the following ingredients:

1 cup butter, softened
1 cup white sugar
1 cup packed brown sugar
2 eggs
2 teaspoons vanilla extract
3 cups all-purpose flour
1 teaspoon baking soda
2 teaspoons hot water
$\frac{1}{2}$ teaspoon salt
2 cups semisweet chocolate chips
1 cup chopped walnuts

Directions:
1. Preheat oven to 350 degrees
2. Cream the butter, white sugar, and brown sugar until smooth
3. Beat in eggs, and then add vanilla
4. Dissolve baking soda in hot water
5. Add baking soda and salt to batter
6. Stir in flour, chocolate chips, and nuts
7. Drop by rounded spoonfuls onto ungreased cookie sheet
8. Bake for ten minutes, or until edges are brown

Okay, you've read the recipe. Sounds yummy, right? Let's think about what kinds of questions will lead us to the essential information. What is it that we need to know so we can make the cookies?

What ingredients do we need?
How much of each ingredient do we need?
What do we do first?
What temperature should the oven be?
When do we add the nuts?
What do we bake the cookies on?
How long do we bake them?

Go back and take a look at the recipe once more. See if you can spot the answers to the questions.

Here are our questions, along with the answers from our recipe:

What ingredients do we need?
butter, white sugar, brown sugar, eggs, vanilla extract, flour, baking soda, hot water, salt, chocolate chips, and walnuts

How much of each ingredient do we need?
1 cup of butter, 1 cup of white sugar, 1 cup of brown sugar, 2 eggs, 2 teaspoons vanilla extract, 3 cups flour, 1 teaspoon baking soda, 2 teaspoons hot water, $\frac{1}{2}$ teaspoon salt, 2 cups chocolate chips, 1 cup walnuts

What do we do first?
Preheat the oven.

What temperature should the oven be?
350 degrees

When do we add the nuts?
after the baking soda and salt, along with the flour and chocolate chips

What do we bake the cookies on?
ungreased cookie sheets

How long do we bake them for?

ten minutes

Again, it's as simple as carefully combing through the passage and extracting all the essential information. The trick is to be an active reader and to really get into the passage. Be curious. Ask yourself questions. There's a reason the author wrote the passage to begin with. There's always information being communicated to the reader. That makes sense, doesn't it? Otherwise, what's the point?

PRACTICE LAP

Read the passage and then answer the questions to practice finding the basic information.

> On Friday afternoon at 4:30 P.M., the fire department was called to Washington Park because of a report of a cat stuck in a tree. When they arrived, they found an orange tabby in a high branch of the oak tree in the center of the park. A crowd had gathered around the tree, with everyone looking up to keep track of the cat. Kathy Green, who had called the fire department, told one of the firefighters that she saw the cat run up the tree. It was being chased by a golden retriever that had gotten loose from his leash. Kathy and some of her friends tried to get the cat down by calling to it and offering it food, but when they saw it wasn't working, Kathy called the fire department. The firefighters were able to rescue the cat by climbing up a ladder.

1. Who was in the tree?
   a. Kathy's friend Marge
   b. Kathy
   c. Kathy's cat
   d. an orange tabby cat

2. How did it get in the tree?

    a. A dog chased it up the tree.

    b. It was chasing a bird in the tree.

    c. It was hiding from its owner.

    d. Kathy's friend put it in the tree.

3. Where did the incident occur?

    a. Pebble Beach

    b. Thompson Square Park

    c. Washington Park

    d. Lincoln Center

4. When did the incident occur?

    a. Sunday morning at 9:00 A.M.

    b. Friday afternoon at 4:30 P.M.

    c. this evening

    d. last night at 10:15 P.M.

5. Who called the fire department?

    a. Kathy Green

    b. Kathy's friend

    c. a member of the crowd

    d. a Washington Park ranger

6. What did Kathy and her friends do to try to get the cat down?

    a. climbed up the tree

    b. called to it

    c. offered it food

    d. b and c

7. What kind of tree did the cat climb?

    a. maple

    b. pine

    c. elm

    d. oak

8. What kind of dog chased the cat up the tree?
   a. Jack Russell terrier
   b. Labrador retriever
   c. golden retriever
   d. poodle

9. How were the firefighters able to rescue the cat?
   a. climbing up a ladder
   b. sounding a horn
   c. calling to it
   d. offering it food

10. What color was the cat in the tree?
   a. calico
   b. black
   c. orange
   d. gray

Check your answers on page 13.

LET'S RECAP

Reading comprehension is about understanding what you read. To do that, you need to uncover the basic information in the text you're reading. To find the basics, you break the text down into smaller bits so it's easier to manage. Ask yourself questions: "What's being discussed?" "Who's involved?" "When did something happen?" If it's helpful, make notes in the margins, circle, or underline text you think might be important.

Just remember to be an active reader—read each sentence carefully and think about what you're reading!

ANSWERS

1. **d.** An orange tabby cat was in the tree.
2. **a.** A dog chased the cat up the tree.
3. **c.** The incident occurred in Washington Park.
4. **b.** The incident occurred on Friday afternoon at 4:30 P.M.
5. **a.** Kathy Green called the fire department.
6. **d.** Kathy and her friends tried to get the cat down by calling to it and offering it food.
7. **d.** The cat climbed an oak tree.
8. **c.** The dog that chased the cat up the tree was a golden retriever.
9. **a.** The firefighters were able to rescue the cat by climbing up a ladder.
10. **c.** The cat in the tree was orange.

Finding the Main Idea

Just like speaking, writing is a form of communication. When you read a passage, the author of that passage is trying to tell you something. Otherwise, why would he or she go to the trouble of writing it? What the author is attempting to communicate to you is called the main idea of the passage. Simply put, the **main idea** is what a passage is mostly about!

Remember the question words in the previous chapter? Well, now's the time to think about that *why* question: Why is the subject of the passage even being discussed in the first place? In other words, what's the point? What does the author want me to know? Asking yourself why is a step in the right direction to finding out the point, or main idea.

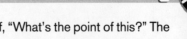

PACE YOURSELF

NEXT TIME YOU read, ask yourself, "What's the point of this?" The answer will be very closely related to the main idea of the text.

SUBJECT VERSUS MAIN IDEA

Sometimes the subject of a passage and the main idea get confused. Let's talk about the difference. The **subject** is what the passage is about. For example:

> Before a raindrop finds its way to the ground, it has already been on a long journey. Raindrops begin as water molecules that are in the earth's oceans, lakes, streams, and other bodies of water. As the sun heats the water, the molecules are evaporated up into the clouds. When there are a lot of water molecules gathered in the clouds, they get heavy and fall to the earth as raindrops. Some of those raindrops fall into the earth's oceans, lakes, and streams and the process begins all over again.

The subject of the passage is rain. It's *about* rain. But the main idea is not just what the passage is *about*; it's what the author *says about* the subject. So, if the subject is rain, what do you think the main idea would be? Reread the passage and see if you can figure out what is being *said about* rain.

Now that you've read it again, think about it. The author explains how water molecules evaporate into the air and form rain that falls and then starts the trip up again. So, the main idea would be something like how rain forms or the rain cycle.

The main idea is, quite literally, the central idea of a passage. All the rest of the text is made up of details that support, or tell more about, that main idea.

Remember:

> *subject* = what the passage is about
> *main idea* = what is said about the subject
> *detail* = information in other sentences that support, or tell more about, the main idea

Let's look at another passage and see if we can distinguish the subject from the main idea.

> In a lot of ways, having a digital camera is better than having a camera with film. For one thing, you can take many more pictures with a digital camera than you can with film. The digital camera holds

the pictures on a small memory card. And because film takes up more space than the memory card, digital cameras are often smaller and easier to fit in a bag or pocket. In addition, a digital camera can be plugged directly into a computer, allowing the user to upload the pictures right after taking them and passing them on via e-mail. Film must be taken in to be developed, which is not only a slower process, but also ends up costing more money.

What's the subject of the passage? In other words, what's it about? That's easy, it's about cameras. But the main idea is a bit trickier. Again, the main idea is what is being *said about* the subject. So, what's being said about digital cameras and film cameras? Read the passage again and see if you can figure out what the main idea is.

One way to determine the main idea is to ask yourself, "What's the point?" and "Why does the author want me to know?" Well, the author seems to be expressing a preference for digital cameras over cameras that use film and giving details to explain why digital cameras are better. So, the main idea could be expressed as follows: Digital cameras are better. Of course, there are other ways to say it, but this is the main idea. Everything else in the passage supports one central, or main, idea.

CAUTION!

BE CAREFUL. SOMETIMES the subject and main idea are very similar. Just remember that the main idea may include the subject, but will need support from details.

INSIDE TRACK

OFTEN THE MAIN idea is stated in the first sentence, so always check that sentence first.

PRACTICE LAP

Identify whether the following statements are a *subject* or a *main idea*.

1. hiccups and other ailments

2. why hiccups occur

3. how to sew on a button

4. buttons, snaps, and hooks

5. why apples are healthy

Check your answers on page 23.

TOPIC SENTENCES

Usually, the main idea of a passage is expressed in the **topic sentence**. Knowing this helps you identify the main idea. Usually, the topic sentence is the first sentence of a passage, but not always. To find it, here's what you do: Find a sentence that needs support. If all the other sentences support a sentence, then it's your topic sentence!

FUEL FOR THOUGHT

THE LONGEST SUSPENSION bridge in the world is the Akashi-Kaikyo Bridge in Japan. It spans 6,529 feet without any support from underneath.

For example, here's a sentence that doesn't need any help:

It's hot.

This is just a basic statement. It might be evidence for some greater issue, but we don't know that because it's all by itself. But here's a statement that does need help:

It can be dangerous to exercise in an atmosphere of extreme heat.

This isn't just your basic statement; it's an idea that needs some support. For example, how does the heat make it dangerous? What could happen to you if you exercise in those conditions? More explanation is definitely needed.

So you should remember that a topic sentence

➡ is often at the beginning of a passage
➡ is a sentence that needs support
➡ usually expresses the main idea of the passage

CAUTION!

DON'T GET HUNG up on the idea of a topic sentence being the first sentence, because sometimes it won't be!

PRACTICE LAP

Identify whether or not the following sentences are *topic sentences*.

6. Glass bottles can be recycled.

7. It is important to vote in local elections.

8. Some people need glasses to help them see clearly.

9. Rats are a kind of rodent.

10. Art classes should be mandatory.

Check your answers on page 23.

IMPLIED MAIN IDEA

Sometimes an author will not explicitly state his or her main idea. It seems strange: Why wouldn't writers want readers to know what the main idea is? Well, they *do* want the reader to know. Sometimes they just don't feel it's necessary to spell it out so clearly. You'll see this often in literature, where stylistic elements make it more important to *imply* the main idea rather than just come right out and say it.

FUEL FOR THOUGHT

HAVE YOU EVER listened to someone tell a story and thought to yourself, "What is the point of this?" It is probably because you didn't hear the main idea explicitly stated.

How to Find It

So, if it's not explicitly stated anywhere in the passage, how do you find out what it is? What you're going to do is look for clues. Think about what you have to work with. You don't have the main idea, but you do have the support for the main idea, so work backward. Read all the sentences and ask yourself, "What main idea are all these sentences supporting?" Look at the following paragraph.

> Mrs. Framingham arrives at school early on Monday mornings so that she can set up her room for the week. Each week, she creates a new theme for her classroom to inspire her art students. Sometimes the theme will be people, and she'll hang portraits all over the room. Then she'll ask her students to draw portraits of each other and even themselves. When Mrs. Framingham teaches her students about sculpture, she takes them on an in-school field trip and carefully points out sculptural elements of the school's architecture and furniture.

As you might have noticed, this paragraph has no topic sentence. So how do you know what the main idea is? Be a detective. Ask yourself what all of the evidence in the paragraph could be supporting. Here's what we know: Mrs. Framingham arrives early on Monday morning. She seems to spend a lot of time thinking about how to inspire her students and uses creative ideas to help them learn. Based on this evidence, the main idea of the paragraph seems to be that Mrs. Framingham is a very dedicated teacher. This seems to be the point of the paragraph. When there is no topic sentence to explicitly state the main idea, you just want to uncover the point: What is it that the author is trying to say with regard to Mrs. Framingham?

FUEL FOR THOUGHT

SHERLOCK HOLMES IS a famous fictional detective created by the author Sir Arthur Conan Doyle. Be a detective like him and investigate what all of the evidence in a paragraph you read could be supporting.

PACE YOURSELF

PRACTICE WORKING BACKWARD by using the following three points of support to create a main idea:

➥ You can be social with your friends at the pool.
➥ Going swimming helps you cool off on a hot day.
➥ Being out in the sun provides your body with vitamin D.

PRACTICE LAP

Read the following passage and then answer the questions.

> If you ask campers at Sunshine Day Camp what they did at camp on any particular day, they may answer that they went swimming or canoeing or that they played tag in the field. These are a few of the activities that Sunshine Day Camp provides, but not the ones of which the camp staff is most proud. The staff at Sunshine Day Camp meets once a week to brainstorm ways to teach the campers new skills. Their latest idea was a camp bake sale, where all the items sold were made at camp by the campers themselves. One whole day of camp that week was dedicated to teaching the campers how to bake.

11. What kinds of activities does Sunshine Day Camp provide?

12. What does the staff do once a week?

13. How is the bake sale different from other camp activities?

14. How does the staff feel about activities like the bake sale?

15. What is the main idea of this passage?

Check your answers on page 23.

LET'S RECAP

Basically, the main idea of any piece of writing is the point that the author is making. So your task is to find out what that point is. To accomplish this task, you need to be able to differentiate between a subject and a main idea, because when you find the main idea, you've found the point. The subject of a passage is merely what is being talked about. What is being discussed? The main idea of a passage is what is being said about that subject. This is what you're looking to find out.

Oftentimes the main idea of a passage can be found in a topic sentence. A topic sentence will usually be at the beginning of a passage and will be a general idea that needs other ideas to support it. As you can see, identifying topic sentences can be a useful tool in finding the main idea.

But what happens if there isn't a topic sentence and nowhere in the passage is the main idea explicitly stated? How do you find it? You need to ask yourself, "What is the author's point?" Use the information you do have to lead you to the main idea. Determine what larger idea all the smaller ideas seem to support.

ANSWERS

1. subject

   Hiccups and other ailments is a general phrase, but doesn't lend itself to being supported by other ideas. It's not making a clear statement.

2. main idea

   Why hiccups occur is an idea that needs some support. If you were to write an explanation for why hiccups occur, you would need reasons explaining why they occur. Other ideas revolve around the statement *why hiccups occur.*

3. main idea

   How to sew on a button is a main idea and not just a subject because it needs more support. A reader would need to know the steps involved in sewing on a button.

4. subject

   Buttons, snaps, and hooks describes a subject and not a main idea because there are no other ideas that revolve around it. There is no more to be said about it.

5. main idea

   Apples are healthy is a main idea because the reader needs to know why apples are healthy. A statement is made about apples and more support is needed to back up the statement.

6. not a topic sentence

   Glass bottles can be recycled is a fairly specific statement that doesn't need any support and is more likely used as support for a more general idea.

8 Express Review Guides: READING COMPREHENSION

7. topic sentence

It is important to vote in local elections is a statement that needs support; for example, why is it important to vote in local elections?

8. not a topic sentence

The fact that *some people need glasses to help them see clearly* is a specific fact that does not express a main idea. It doesn't cry out for support and therefore is not a topic sentence.

9. not a topic sentence

Rats are a kind of rodent is a fact and it does not take a stand or need support in any way. It is not a topic sentence.

10. topic sentence

Art classes should be mandatory is an opinion that needs to be supported. It definitely expresses a main idea, so it is topic sentence.

The answers to questions 11 through 14 can all be found in the passage provided. The passage is shown again here with all of the pertinent information underlined.

If you ask campers at Sunshine Day Camp what they did at camp on any particular day, they may answer that they went <u>swimming or canoeing or that they played tag</u> in the field. These are a few of the activities that Sunshine Day Camp provides, but not the ones of which <u>the camp staff is most proud. The staff at Sunshine Day Camp meets once a week to brainstorm ways to teach the campers new skills. Their latest idea was a camp bake sale</u>, where all the items sold were made at camp by the campers themselves. <u>One whole day of camp that week was dedicated to teaching the campers how to bake</u>.

11. Sunshine Day Camp provides activities like swimming, canoeing, tag, and baking.

12. The staff meets once a week to brainstorm ways to teach the campers new skills.

13. The bake sale is different from other camp activities because it is not a typical camp activity and it teaches the campers new skills.

14. The staff is very proud of activities like the bake sale.

15. The main idea of this passage is that camp does not always have to be just about swimming, canoeing, and typical camp activities. Camp can also be an opportunity for campers to learn new skills.

Even though the main idea is not explicitly stated within the passage, you can infer the main idea from the information you know: The staff is most proud of the bake sale, and they brainstorm each week for activities to teach campers new skills. Therefore, this camp is different from others because it teaches campers new skills.

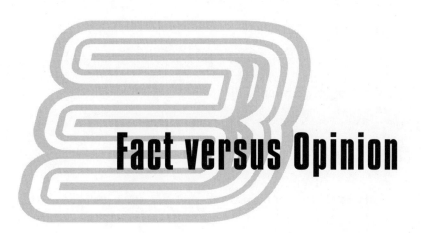

Fact versus Opinion

Why is there a whole chapter in this book dedicated to the differences between fact and opinion? Because it's really important to know the differences in becoming a critical reader . . . and making your way through all the hype you get from the media! You need to be able to separate fact from opinion in just about everything you read or hear. Otherwise, you may inadvertently take as a fact something that is entirely an opinion. And being able to judge the difference can help you logically analyze information based on how well the author supports his or her opinion with the facts. We'll get to that part later, but for now, let's concentrate on what makes a fact or opinion and how to tell the difference between the two.

FUEL FOR THOUGHT

SOMEONE WHO is *gullible* is easily fooled.

WHAT'S A FACT?

A **fact** is something that can be proven to be true and that is not up for debate. A fact is something like this:

A tree is a plant.

or

The Earth has gravitational pull.

or

You're reading an *Express Review Guide.*

Those are facts. They can be proved true. We don't just like to think they're true . . . we know they are!

PACE YOURSELF

WRITE DOWN THREE facts or things you know to be true and that aren't open for debate.

Think about all the things you know are true. It's pretty crazy, isn't it, to think about how many facts you already know? You know how old you are. It's a fact. You know your birthday. It's also a fact. You know lots of other things, like your favorite color, for instance. Even that is a fact. You might think that because you picked it yourself, your favorite color's not a fact, but it is. If you decide that your favorite color from now on will be green, then that's a fact. Think about it. Can it be debated? Can someone come up to you and say, "Nope, I think your favorite color is really yellow"? No. Well, someone could, but your favorite color isn't yellow, because you just decided that it's green! And that's a fact!

WHAT'S AN OPINION?

An **opinion** is something that someone believes. It hasn't been proven to be true and can definitely be debated. Here's an example:

Cookies are delicious.

Even if you're a cookie lover, this is not a fact. Although it's hard to imagine, there are people who don't think cookies are delicious. Therefore, *cookies are delicious* is an opinion or belief that someone might disagree with.

Sometimes you can spot an opinion right away because the author uses phrases like *This reporter believes . . .*, *In my opinion . . .*, or *Many people believe that . . .* But other times, you have to read between the lines to sift out the opinions. Why? An opinion may be based on facts and supported by them, but it's still only a belief. For example:

Cats are good pets.

FUEL FOR THOUGHT

HERE'S A FACT about cats. According to the Humane Society of the United States, 38.4 million U.S. households have at least one cat.

Not everyone would agree with this statement. It's a belief. And it could be supported with facts like these:

Millions of people in the United States have cats.
You don't have to walk cats.
They give themselves baths.
Cats are small and furry.

All this may be true, but the original statement is still just an opinion, not a fact.

Here's what you need to remember:

fact = something that is known to be true

opinion = something that is a belief

PACE YOURSELF

SPEND SOME TIME listening carefully to what people say to you. Are they giving you facts or opinions?

CAUTION!

DON'T BE FOOLED by opinions masquerading as facts. Think carefully about whether something is actually known to be true, or whether it's just what someone thinks.

PRACTICE LAP

Identify each statement as a *fact* or an *opinion*.

1. Coffee doesn't always contain caffeine.

2. It's easier to write with a pen than a pencil.

3. Cell phones should be banned from classrooms.

4. Winter is the best season.

5. The elephant is the largest land mammal.

6. Paper clips are usually metal.

7. It's enjoyable to watch a movie.

Check your answers on page 35.

SUPPORTING OPINIONS WITH FACTS

Part of what makes someone a good writer is the ability to support opinions with facts. To prove a point, the author needs to back up an opinion with real facts. There might be two different topic sentences stating equally valid, but opposing, opinions. As long as each opinion has facts to back it up, both opinions would be reasonable. For example, here's the opinion we just discussed, and an opposing opinion.

> Cats are good pets.
> Cats are not good pets.

We've already gone over some facts that support the first opinion. Here they are again, in case you forgot:

> Millions of people in the United States have cats.
> You don't have to walk cats.
> They give themselves baths.
> Cats are small and furry.

Now here are some facts to support that second opposing opinion:

> Cats don't normally play fetch.
> Cats can be very solitary animals.
> Many people are allergic to cats.
> Some cats may scratch up your furniture.

These are facts that support the opinion that cats aren't good pets. So, as you can see, both opinions can be supported with facts . . . but they're still opinions!

What would happen if a writer tried to support an opinion with other opinions? It might look something like this:

> With regard to the city council's recent discussion on whether the parking lot on Main Street should be turned into a park, I'd like to say that I am heartily in favor of the transformation. Parks are

beautiful. All the trees, grass, and flowers are so relaxing to look at on a sunny afternoon from the seat of a park bench, whereas the parking lot that is currently there is so ugly.

From the first sentence of the passage, we know the author is in favor of turning the parking lot into a park. But what reasons does the author give? Here's what the author uses to support the opinion that the parking lot should be a park:

Reason #1: Parks are beautiful.
Reason #2: Trees, grass, and flowers are relaxing to view.
Reason #3: The parking lot is ugly.

All these reasons are opinions! Maybe some other people don't think parks are beautiful. Maybe someone with allergies couldn't relax near trees and grass. And someone might make an argument regarding the beauty of a parking lot! If each of the author's reasons can be debated, they're not such great support for his or her opinion, are they? The more factual and logical an author's reasons are, the more likely the reader will agree with the opinion. So, it just doesn't make sense to use only opinions to support an opinion! Read the following passage about constructing a new building for a local high school.

My name is Marianne Peterson, and I am a member of the PTA in our school district. I am strongly in favor of constructing a new building for the high school, mostly because the old building is just too small. However, the old building is not only too small, but also ill equipped to accommodate the needs of its students. We need to give our students a better building that is bigger *and* better equipped.

Does Marianne use facts or opinions to support her position? (If you need to, read the passage again and mark it up.) The first step is to identify her reasons. Then you can determine whether they're facts or opinions and if they strengthen or weaken her argument. Here are the two reasons Marianne gives for why she thinks the high school needs a new building:

Reason #1: The current building is too small.

Reason #2: The current building is ill equipped.

Now that we've identified Marianne's reasons, we need to figure out if they are facts or opinions. What do you think? Can what she said be debated? They can, so therefore, they are opinions. It's not hard to imagine that someone would argue that the current building isn't too small, the space just isn't being used wisely, the school isn't ill equipped, and that the teachers just need to make better use of what they have!

So, both of Marianne's reasons can be debated. What does this do to her argument? Well, as we saw in the park example, an argument isn't very strong if it's supported only by opinions. Imagine how much stronger Marianne's argument would be if she could *prove* that the current building was too small. What if she said that according to the community fire code, the building needed two exits for every hundred students and that currently there was only one exit for every hundred students? That one fact would lend a lot of weight to her argument. One good fact can make more of an impact than many opinions.

PACE YOURSELF

WRITE A LETTER to convince a friend to go to the movies with you. First, write the letter using only opinions to back up your argument. Then write the letter using only facts. Read both letters. Which seems like the stronger argument?

Now you know how to tell a fact from an opinion and how facts can support an opinion. Remember, all you have to do is ask yourself whether the statement can be debated or if it can be proven to be true. If it can be debated—if someone else could have an opposing view—then it's an opinion. If it can be proven to be true, then it's a fact.

PRACTICE LAP

Identify each statement as a *fact* or an *opinion*.

8. I get hives when I eat strawberries.

9. Mrs. Booth has been named Teacher of the Year by her students.

10. If it is raining, the best type of shoe to wear is a boot.

11. *Star Wars* is one of the ten best movies of all time.

12. *Star Wars* is on my top ten best movie list.

13. Some people have jobs that enable them to work from home.

14. The Super Bowl is the most exciting football game of the year.

Check your answers on page 35.

LET'S RECAP

Knowing the difference between what's true and what isn't is vital in reading comprehension. A fact is something that can be proven to be true and isn't up for debate; an opinion is a belief that can be debated. As you read, look for facts and opinions and how the author uses them to express a main idea.

Beware of arguments supported only by opinions. When an author proposes an argument, his or her goal is to convince you to have that particular viewpoint. The best way to do this is to support the argument or claim with facts because readers will know that facts are true. Anyone can have any old opinion, but a fact is a fact. Therefore, your ability to differentiate between facts and opinions is essential to understanding the strength and validity of an argument presented to you.

ANSWERS

1. fact

It is a fact that coffee does not always contain caffeine. There is such a thing as decaffeinated coffee, which does not contain caffeine.

2. opinion

Not everyone would agree that it is easier to write with a pen than a pencil. Some people might think it's easier to write with a pencil.

3. opinion

To ban cell phones from classrooms is debatable because of safety issues, so it's not a fact.

4. opinion

Some people might disagree with the statement that winter is the best season. They might prefer spring or summer seasons. All of these preferences are opinions, not facts.

5. fact

It has been proven than elephants are the largest land mammals. This information is stated in encyclopedias, is known to be true, and, therefore, is a fact.

6. fact

Some paper clips aren't made of metal, but most are. This is a fact.

7. opinion

Some people might not think going to a movie is enjoyable. Therefore, those who believe it is enjoyable adhere to this opinion.

8. fact

This one is a bit tricky because you don't know who the *I* is in the sentence. But regardless of who is speaking, the statement is a fact because it is known to be true by the person talking.

9. fact

It is a fact that Mrs. Booth's students named her Teacher of the Year. To think that a particular person should be Teacher of the Year is one's opinion, but Mrs. Booth actually being named Teacher of the Year is something that is not debatable.

10. opinion

Some could disagree with this statement. Perhaps one believes boots are not the best type of shoe to wear in the rain. This is an opinion.

11. opinion

Different people have different opinions about which movie is one of the ten best of all time. It is debatable, and it is an opinion.

12. fact

It can be proven that *Star Wars* is written on one person's top ten best movies list. The fact lies in that the movie could exist on someone's top ten list, and once it is there, it cannot be debated that it is on the list.

13. fact

It is a fact that some people have jobs that enable them to work from home. This can be proved by checking the census or tax records.

14. opinion

Some sports fans may disagree with the statement that the Super Bowl is the most exciting football game of the year. This is an opinion.

Chronological Order

In the next few chapters, we'll be talking about various text structures that writers use to organize their ideas. Don't worry; it may sound like really deep stuff, but it's not. The more you understand about *why* writers do things, the more you get out of what you read. It'll become easier to understand what a writer's trying to communicate once you know why he or she has chosen to use one text structure over another.

First, let's talk about chronological order text structure, and then we'll go over some text to practice. A text in **chronological order** tells a story in sequence. The first thing that happens is told first, and the last thing that happens is told last. Sometimes writers use words that signal the order, such as *first*, *next*, *then*, *last*, *now*, and *finally*. Other times you have to figure out the order from the events themselves. For example, you couldn't leave a party until *after* you've arrived there, and you have to start your homework *before* you can finish it!

Check out the first two sentences of the preceding paragraph for an example of writing in chronological order. Here are the two events listed:

Talk about chronological order

and

Go over some text to practice

As you can see, the first sentence told what would occur first and the second sentence told what would occur second.

Not everything's written in chronological order, but a lot of writing is. Think of directions or instructions. They begin by telling you what to do first and end by telling you what to do last. Travel directions tell you where to start and where you will end. Instructions for putting together a bookcase tell you which pieces to assemble first and end with what the finished bookcase will look like! As far as instructions and directions go, chronological structure is the most effective way of conveying information to the reader.

FUEL FOR THOUGHT

YOU'VE PROBABLY HEARD the expression, "I'm having a flashback." In a story or piece of writing, a **flashback** is an interruption telling you something that happened before that point in the story.

PACE YOURSELF

MAKE A CHRONOLOGICAL list of everything you've done today.

HOW TO SPOT CHRONOLOGICAL ORDER

So, how do you tell if something's written in chronological order? Read to see if

➡ the passage contains time-order clue words
➡ events are listed in the order in which they occurred

Let's look at another passage that uses the chronological-order text structure.

How to Make Chocolate Chip Cookies

Before you start, look over the list of ingredients, and make sure you have everything you need to make the cookies. Once you're sure you have everything you need, preheat the oven to 350 degrees. Then measure out the flour, baking soda, and salt, and put them in a bowl. Set that bowl aside, and in a separate bowl, mix together the butter, sugar, eggs, and vanilla. Next, slowly add the dry ingredients into all the other ingredients, a little bit at a time. After all the dry ingredients are incorporated, fold in the chocolate chips. Then, use a spoon to drop small piles of the dough onto an ungreased cookie sheet, leaving enough space between the piles for the dough to spread out. Finally, bake the cookies for eight to ten minutes or until golden.

INSIDE TRACK

TRY MAKING A list as you read the events mentioned in the passage. The list will help you visualize the order in which things should be done.

Let's assume you've never made chocolate chip cookies before. Then you probably wouldn't know that chocolate chips are folded in *after* the other ingredients are mixed. So we'll rely on your powers of observation.

What words in the recipe seem like clues to the order of the steps for making cookies? Here's the passage again, with some of those words underlined:

How to Make Chocolate Chip Cookies

<u>Before</u> you start, look over the list of ingredients, and make sure you have everything you need to make the cookies. <u>After</u> you're sure you have everything you need, preheat the oven to 350 degrees. <u>Then</u> measure out the flour, baking soda, and salt, and put them in a bowl. Set that bowl aside, and <u>then</u> in a separate bowl, mix together the butter, sugar, eggs, and vanilla. <u>Next</u>, slowly add the dry ingredients into all the other ingredients, a little bit at a time. <u>After</u> all the dry ingredients are incorporated, fold in the chocolate chips. <u>Then</u>, use a spoon to drop small piles of the dough onto an ungreased cookie sheet, leaving enough space between the piles for the dough to spread out. <u>Finally</u>, bake the cookies for eight to ten minutes or until golden.

Notice that all the words underlined are **transitional words** that indicate the order in which things are supposed to occur. These words make the paragraph cohesive and are often used in chronological-order text structure. Here's a list of words and phrases to look for:

first	soon	now
second	after	before
third	next	during
while	then	meanwhile
when	in the meantime	finally
as soon as	at last	eventually
immediately	suddenly	prior to

CAUTION!

DON'T RELY SOLELY on clue words and phrases. Make sure you read the words in context.

PRACTICE LAP

Put a number from 1–5 next to each sentence to indicate the order in which each event happened chronologically.

_____ Soon the principal arrived and told us it was just a drill.

_____ We started talking, and during our conversation, the fire alarm went off.

_____ As soon as the alarm stopped ringing, we all went back inside.

_____ When I first got to school, I ran into my friend Rachel in the hallway.

_____ So, we immediately walked toward the door I had just come in and followed the rest of the students to the parking lot.

Check your answers on page 46.

CAUSE AND EFFECT

Many times, passages you read have a **cause-and-effect** text structure. The author tells you about something that happens and why it happens. In fact, a passage may contain more than one cause-and-effect scenario.

cause = person, thing, or event that makes something happen

effect = what happens due to the action of a person, thing, or event

FUEL FOR THOUGHT

A *SCENARIO* **IS** a sequence of events.

PACE YOURSELF

WRITE DOWN THREE cause-and-effect scenarios that happened in your life this week.

When text is written in chronological order, it's easier to spot the causes and effects because causes occur *before* effects. Read the following passage and you'll see:

> A recent change in grading policies prompted the school principal, Mr. Rivera, to hold an assembly during fourth period on Tuesday. The assembly began on time, and the principal began to discuss the new grading system. He had been speaking for about ten minutes when he noticed a girl in the second row blowing a bubble with her gum. Because chewing gum was a violation of school rules and Mr. Rivera thought that it was rude to be blowing a bubble while he was speaking, he became distracted and lost his train of thought. It was only a momentary distraction, however, and he continued with the assembly. Before it was over, he thought of a new rule, and announced to the students in the auditorium that anyone caught chewing gum in school would have to write him a one-page essay explaining the basis for the no-chewing-gum rule. The students all groaned, and the assembly was dismissed.

Did you spot the cause-and-effect relationships in the passage? The first is in the very first sentence. The recent change in grading policies *caused* Mr. Rivera to hold an assembly. In the sentence, *prompted* is just another way of saying *caused*.

cause = recent change in grading policies

effect = Mr. Rivera holds an assembly

Here is the next cause-and-effect relationship in the passage:

cause = girl blowing a chewing-gum bubble

effect = Mr. Rivera loses his train of thought

As you can see, the passage is written in chronological order, with events listed in the time order in which they happened, so each cause is followed by its effect or vice versa. Can you spot another cause-and-effect relationship in the passage? There are a couple of them.

cause = the girl making Mr. Rivera lose his train of thought

effect = Mr. Rivera creating a new punishment for gum chewers

cause = Mr. Rivera creates a new punishment for gum chewers

effect = the students groan

CAUTION!

CAUSE-AND-EFFECT relationships are easy to spot when text is written in chronological order, but be careful if the author is using a different text structure. Causes may not always be followed closely by their effects.

PRACTICE LAP

For each sentence, explain in your own words the *cause* and the *effect*.

6. The darkening sky caused Jamal to bring his umbrella.

7. One of the effects of the new stop sign is that there have been fewer accidents.

8. Snow on the tracks caused the trains to be late.

9. Dan's dripping ice cream cone caused him to need more napkins.

10. An effect of adding more sugar is that the cookies are sweeter.

Check your answers on page 46.

Cause and effect is much more difficult to identify if a passage isn't written in chronological order. Most likely, you won't find text like these two examples:

> The temperature fell below freezing, and the effect was that the water on the sidewalk froze.

> The cause of the water freezing on the sidewalk was the temperature falling below freezing.

That would be too obvious. You're much more likely to come across a sentence like this:

> The temperature fell so low last night that passersby were holding onto streetlamps and mailboxes in an attempt not to slip on the ice.

In all three sentences, the cause-and-effect relationship is the same. The cause is the below-freezing temperature and the effect is that water on the sidewalk froze. Because we know that water becomes ice when the temperature falls below freezing and we know people slip on ice, we can infer the cause and effect without it being explicitly stated. Just ask yourself which things made something happen and which things happened as a result of something else.

PACE YOURSELF

THINK OF SOMETHING you did today. Now think of the causes and effects of that action.

PRACTICE LAP

For each sentence, identify in your own words the *cause* and the *effect*.

11. In order to keep up with his friend, John had to run faster.

12. It was so loud in the theater that I couldn't hear the movie.

13. Because Tom was in a hurry this morning, he didn't eat any breakfast.

14. A hiking map was created for nearby Hyde Peak, because the community had complained that there was no way to plan their trips before setting out for the mountain.

15. Crooks' Books, Shadeville's mystery book shop, had a sale this week to honor the tenth anniversary of their opening.

Check your answers on page 46.

LET'S RECAP

Chronological order is one text structure that authors use when they write. When text is placed in chronological order, it is written in the order in which events occurred—it tells what happened first in time order, and what happened last in time order. There are two ways to spot text written in chronological order: Notice if events are written about in the order in which they occurred, and look for clue time words and phrases in the passage.

Keep in mind that when things happen, they usually affect other things. A cause makes something happen. An effect is what happens as a result. Spotting cause-and-effect relationships is a big part of reading comprehension. Knowing how things affect one another boosts your ability to understand what you read. If the text is in chronological order, it's easy to pick out the causes and effects because a cause happens before its effect. If the text isn't in chronological order, just think about which things made something happen and which things were results of something else that took place. Those are your causes and effects!

ANSWERS

1. 4
2. 2
3. 5
4. 1
5. 3
6. cause = darkening sky

   effect = Jamal brings his umbrella

   The darkening sky was the cause of Jamal bringing his umbrella. Jamal bringing his umbrella was the effect of the darkening sky.
7. cause = new stop sign

   effect = fewer accidents

   The new stop sign is the cause of fewer accidents. Fewer accidents are the effect of the new stop sign.
8. cause = snow on the tracks

   effect = trains were late

   The snow on the tracks was the cause of the trains being late. The trains' lateness was the effect of snow on the tracks.
9. cause = dripping ice cream

   effect = needs more napkins

   The dripping ice cream was the cause of Dan needing more napkins. The need for more napkins was the effect of the dripping ice cream.
10. cause = adding more sugar

    effect = sweeter cookies

    Adding more sugar was the cause of the cookies being sweeter. The cookies' increased sweetness was the effect of adding more sugar.
11. cause = friend runs faster

    effect = John runs faster

    John had to keep up with his friend, so his friend running faster was the cause of John running faster. John running faster was the effect of his friend running faster.
12. cause = loudness in the theater

    effect = not hearing the movie

    The loudness of the theater was the cause of not being able to hear the movie. Not hearing the movie was the effect of it being loud in the theater.

13. cause = being in a hurry

effect = not eating breakfast

Being in a hurry was the cause of Tom not eating breakfast. Not eating breakfast was the effect of being in a hurry.

14. cause = complaints from the community

effect = creation of a hiking map

Complaints from the community were the cause of the creation of a hiking map. The creation of a hiking map was the effect of complaints from the community.

15. cause = tenth anniversary

effect = sale

The bookstore's tenth anniversary was the cause of the store having a sale. The sale was the effect of the bookstore celebrating its tenth anniversary.

Order of Importance

Another type of text structure that some writers use is order of importance. While chronological order text structure is based on time order, or sequence, this text structure is based on the importance of the information in the passage.

You probably don't even realize you do it, but when you read, you often make decisions about what's important and what isn't. Maybe you don't eat fish, so when you look at a restaurant menu, you immediately skip over all the seafood entrees. This is an example of making a decision about what's important to you in something you read. Writers know that readers make these decisions, so writers often choose to structure their text by putting in the most important stuff they want the reader to know in such a way that the reader will most likely read it and not skip over it.

INSIDE TRACK

IDENTIFYING WHAT THE writer thinks is important gives you a valuable insight into his or her motivations for writing.

Order of importance text structuring can be done in two ways:

> most important ——→ least important

> least important ——→ most important

Let's look at each way of writing something in order of importance and think about why a writer might choose to use one way over the other.

PACE YOURSELF

WE ALL HAVE something that's important to us. Think of something that's really important to you.

FUEL FOR THOUGHT

READING COMPREHENSION IS an important tool to help you understand the world around you.

MOST IMPORTANT ——→ LEAST IMPORTANT

There are a few reasons why a writer might choose to begin with the most important point and end with the least. It could be for stylistic purposes because it certainly makes more of an impact to start with the most important thing. Mystery stories are often told in this way, purely for the impact it makes on the reader. Imagine a story in which someone disappears or some other crime is committed in the first scene. The rest of the story might tell all the events that led up to that main, dramatic incident. See how starting with the most important thing can make an impact on readers and draw them into the story?

Read the following opening paragraph to a story:

> Keisha didn't know it yet, but she was about to faint suddenly. She
> didn't know this yet either, but two minutes after she had fainted,
> she would wake up where she had fallen on the dewy grass and not
> remember that her name was Keisha.

Are you intrigued? If you are, it's probably because the story starts with such
a dramatic event. Of course, there are questions. What will cause Keisha to
faint . . . and why won't she remember her name? The answers will be
unveiled later in the story, but Keisha fainting is the most important event.
It's the thing that grabs the reader and says, "Read on!" It's the incident on
which the rest of the story will attempt to shed some light. So, now you can
see why especially in fiction, going from most important information to least
important information can be a powerful, dramatic tool.

PACE YOURSELF

RANK THE FOLLOWING in order of importance to you, from most
important ———▶ least important. Rank from 1–3, with 1 being the
most important.

_____ getting good grades in school
_____ having a lot of friends
_____ playing sports

Beginning with the most important thing can affect a reader in other ways,
too. Maybe the writer wants to impress readers by offering his or her best
thought right up front. This might immediately capture the readers' attention and make the rest of the text seem all the more believable.

What if you met someone on the street and asked the person a medical
question? For example, "Why do people get the hiccups?" So you ask this to
a random person, who gives you an answer and walks away. Then you ask
someone else. Now you've asked two people the same question. Each gave

you a different answer, but there's another major difference between the people. The first person just gave an answer and told you nothing about himself. The second began by telling you that she was a doctor. Whose answer are you more likely to believe? You'd probably believe the doctor. Well, it's the same when writers put their best, most important, and impressive information first. They sound believable.

Unfortunately for writers, there's always a risk that a reader won't be interested in what the writer has to say and won't read the whole thing. Writers are aware of this, so they might structure their writing in order of importance, placing the most important point first to make sure readers at least realize what the most important point is. It's sort of like road signs that show:

SLOW—Construction Ahead

The most important information is for you to slow down. If you don't read the whole sign, at least you know to decrease speed. Now this is a very simple example, but it helps you see why some writers choose the most important ⟶ least important text structure!

CAUTION!

EVEN IF SOMETHING'S written in most important ⟶ least important, you should still read the whole passage. The least important point to the author might be a more important one to you!

PACE YOURSELF

FIND A NEWSPAPER article and determine whether it's written with the most important information first or the most important information last.

Take a minute to read the following passage, written with the most important ⟶ least important text structure.

> There are many benefits to reading more often. First and fore-most, reading more will broaden your understanding of yourself and of other people. It will also introduce you to new information and ideas. Furthermore, it will improve your overall reading com-prehension, so you'll begin to understand more of what you read. In addition, reading more will improve your vocabulary and increase your reading speed.

You can tell by the phrase *first and foremost* that the most important benefit of reading is listed first. It's the broadening of your understanding of your-self and others. Each of the other benefits is stated in decreasing importance. Generally, a writer will want you to know which point's most important, so all you have to do is carefully observe the words to figure out what the author thinks is most important. He or she will often use words like *first and foremost*, *most importantly*, *most critically*, or even *best of all*.

FUEL FOR THOUGHT

THE CREDITS FOR movies and television shows are structured in order of importance. Ever notice how the most popular actors' names are always first?

LEAST IMPORTANT ⟶ MOST IMPORTANT

Now you know why writers might put the most important thing first, so let's figure out why they might do the opposite, by putting the least important idea first.

You've probably heard the old expression, *save the best for last*. Well, that's the basic idea for writing text with the most important point at the end. Like the most important ——► least important form, the least important ——► most important form is also used to create a dramatic effect. For example, maybe the writer is preparing the reader for a big dramatic ending, so you read and read and build up expectations (similar to waiting for the punch line of a joke).

PACE YOURSELF

THINK OF A time when you saved the best for last.

Saving the best for last is most often used as a tool to build an argument. Writers use the least important ——► most important text structure to convince readers about certain ideas or actions. This is effective because as the writer builds more and more reasons why the reader should agree, and caps it off with one final, most-important reason, the reader is more likely to be convinced.

INSIDE TRACK

THINK OF THE least important ——► most important structure as a snowball. As the snowball rolls down the hill, it gathers more and more snow, just like the argument gathers more and more strength.

Remember the passage that was written in most important ——► least important text structures? Well, here it is, written in least important ——► most important:

> There are many benefits to reading more often. First, it will increase your reading speed, so that you can read more in less time. Second, it will improve your vocabulary. Third, it will improve your overall reading comprehension, and you'll understand more of what you read. In addition, reading more will introduce you to

new information and ideas. Most importantly, it will broaden your understanding of yourself and of other people.

The phrase in this passage that should tip you off to the fact that it is written in the least important ⟶ most important structure is *most importantly*. The phrase comes in the last sentence and introduces the most important point of the passage. This version of the passage, unlike the other, seems to build an argument for why a person should read more often, instead of merely stating the benefits. Although the content is the same, when the importance of each point gets greater as you read, you get a sense that the author is building up to an even bigger point. Instead of just being a passage about the benefits of reading, written in this text structure, the passage seems to become an argument for why you should read more often. Read each passage again and see if you can sense the difference.

> There are many benefits to reading more often. First and foremost, reading more will broaden your understanding of yourself and of other people. It will also introduce you to new information and ideas. Furthermore, it will improve your overall reading comprehension, so you'll begin to understand more of what you read. In addition, reading more will improve your vocabulary and increase your reading speed.

> There are many benefits to reading more often. First, it will increase your reading speed, so that you can read more in less time. Second, it will improve your vocabulary. Third, it will improve your overall reading comprehension, and you'll understand more of what you read. In addition, reading more will introduce you to new information and ideas. Most importantly, it will broaden your understanding of yourself and of other people.

As you can see, order of importance can be a useful text structure, whether it's most important ⟶ least important, or the other way around. Either way, it's helpful to be able to identify which structure the writer is using so you can better understand what you read. It helps you get inside the author's head and figure out his or her motive for writing the text. And that's an important step toward understanding the ideas contained in the writing itself.

CAUTION!

MAKE SURE YOU observe what the author thinks is most important, not what you think is most important.

PRACTICE LAP

Read the passage and answer the questions that follow.

When you're at the beach, it's best to swim only when there's a lifeguard on duty. First of all, lifeguards can be good resources. So, if you and your family or friends have any questions or concerns about any water safety issues, a lifeguard could provide you with the answers you need. Also, lifeguards are more aware than the average swimmer of what the conditions of the ocean are at any given time. They might determine that the undercurrent is too strong to swim. In this way, lifeguards can help ensure that your swim in the ocean is a safe one. Most importantly, it's best to swim only when a lifeguard is on duty, because if you should end up needing rescuing or CPR, then a lifeguard is there to help.

1. Identify the three reasons why it's best to swim only when there's a lifeguard on duty.

2. In what order are the reasons presented?

3. Which reason is most important?

4. How can you tell that this is the most important reason?

5. Where in the passage is the most important reason stated?

6. What writing structure is represented here?

7. Why do you think the author chose this particular type of structure?

Check your answers below.

LET'S RECAP

Some passages you come across may be written in order of importance. This means the ideas discussed will be ranked in order of how important they are to the author. This can be done in two different ways: most important idea first and least important last, or least important idea first and most important last. By being an active reader and carefully observing what's written in the text, you can determine if an author is using the order of importance text structure and in which order. Look for key words and phrases that point the way.

Why would a writer use the order-of-importance text structure? An author might present facts from most important ⟶ least important to make an immediate impact and pull the reader in, or to make sure people who don't read a whole passage will still get the most important information. An author might use the least important ⟶ most important structure to build suspense or build up to the main point of a message. Either way, identifying this text structure gives you a better understanding of what the author is trying to communicate.

ANSWERS

1. Three reasons why it's best to swim only when there's a lifeguard on duty are:
   1. Lifeguards are good resources.
   2. Lifeguards are more aware of swimming conditions.
   3. A lifeguard could be a lifesaver.

2. This is the order in which the reasons are presented:
   1. Lifeguards are good resources.
   2. Lifeguards are more aware of swimming conditions.
   3. A lifeguard could be a lifesaver.

3. The most important reason is that a lifeguard could save your life.

4. You can tell that this is the most important reason because it follows the phrase *most importantly*.

5. The most important reason is the last reason stated.

6. The text structure is least important ⟶ most important.

7. The author probably chose this text structure because the most important reason makes an impact at the end. The author may think readers are already aware of the most important reason because it's well known. So, starting with lesser-known reasons might make readers keep reading.

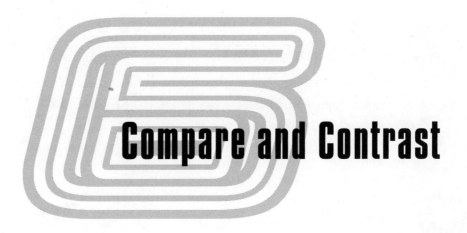

Compare and Contrast

he next text structure we'll investigate is **compare and contrast**. First of all, what is it? Simply put, to compare things, you look for ways they are alike; to contrast things, you look for how they are different.

A writer may have several reasons for using a compare-and-contrast text structure. Sometimes it gives readers a new perspective on things. So you can read a passage and think to yourself, "Wow, I never thought to compare those two things!" Writers love to use the wow factor, but it's not the only reason to use this text structure. Suppose a writer wants to tell readers which fruits and vegetables are the healthiest choices. The writer might compare and contrast the vitamin and mineral content of various fruits and vegetables. Then, for example, readers will know which food to choose that contains more vitamin A.

We all compare and contrast out of habit, all the time. We check out two pairs of pants in a clothing store to decide which to buy (*both are brown, but one has more pockets*). In the grocery store, we carefully compare apples (*both are red, but one is firmer than another and one has a bruise*). We compare and contrast people (*He looks like Brad Pitt!*) and objects (*The clouds look like giant cotton balls*). As we observe the world around us and make everyday decisions, we constantly compare and contrast. (How do you think this chapter compares with the last one so far?)

EVER HEARD THE expression *It's like apples and oranges*? It's used to refer to two things that are very different. The basis for the expression is the contrast between apples and oranges.

PACE YOURSELF

PICK TWO OBJECTS and make a list of their similarities and differences.

Just so that we're clear on which means which, comparing highlights similarities while contrasting highlights differences.

compare = similarities

contrast = differences

PACE YOURSELF

PICK TWO ITEMS that you can see from where you are sitting. Make a list of all the ways they are alike. Make another list of all the ways they are different.

The main idea of a passage will most likely tell if things are being compared or contrasted. Read the following passage to determine what is being compared or contrasted.

Some might say that, in a lot of ways, going to school is similar to having a job. Like a job, attending school requires that you show up at a certain time, and if you are late, there are consequences. Also, in the same way that at work you find yourself having to get along with other people, at school you may have to work on a homework assignment with students who aren't necessarily your friends. At a job, there are frequently projects to complete by certain deadlines. Similarly, at school, teachers assign homework that is due on a specific day. In these ways, going to school is very much like having a job.

You probably noticed that two things were being compared in the passage. The first sentence, which is also the topic sentence, tells you that going to school is similar to having a job. The rest of the passage gives some examples of how the two are similar.

Writers use words and phrases to signal that they are comparing or contrasting. You probably noticed some in the passage you just read. Here is a list of words and phrases writers use to signal that two things are being compared or contrasted.

Comparing	Contrasting
similarly	but
likewise	on the other hand
like	however
just as	conversely
both	yet
in the same way	on the contrary
in common	nevertheless
also	different
and	although

PRACTICE LAP

For each sentence, identify whether something is being *compared* or *contrasted*.

1. Reading is very much like watching a movie in the way that it can take you to a different place in your mind.

2. Although they share a word in their name, snow-skiing and water-skiing are completely different sports.

3. Laughter is medicine for the sad.

4. Mints and chewing gum have a lot in common.

5. Running and swimming each have a very different impact on a person's body.

6. Dollar coins have yet to see mainstream use, because they are so similar to the other coins that are often cumbersome to carry around.

7. Both bricks and stones can be used for construction in similar ways.

8. A laptop computer has some advantages that a desktop model does not have.

Check your answers on page 67.

Within the compare-and-contrast test structure, there are two different **substructures**. A writer could compare and contrast using the point-by-point method, or by using a block style.

FUEL FOR THOUGHT

A VENN DIAGRAM is a graphic organizer that uses overlapping circles to visually illustrate similarities and differences.

POINT-BY-POINT METHOD

The **point-by-point** method compares or contrasts two things, characteristic by characteristic. For example, the passage you read that compared going to school with having a job was written in the point-by-point structure. Let's look at that passage.

Some might say that, in a lot of ways, going to school is similar to having a job. Like a job, attending school requires that you show up at a certain time and if you are late, there are consequences. Also, in the same way that at work, you find yourself having to get along with other people, at school you may have to work on a homework assignment with students who aren't necessarily your friends. At a job, there are frequently projects to complete by certain deadlines. Similarly, at school teachers assign homework that is due on a specific day. In these ways, going to school is very much like having a job.

The first thing the author discusses is being on time. At a job, you have to be on time and at school you have to be on time, too. Then the author discusses getting along with others you have to work with at a job and also at school. Do you see the pattern? Each aspect of having a job is directly compared to that same aspect of going to school.

BLOCK METHOD

The **block method** is discusses one thing fully and then the other thing fully. Using this method, the comparison between school and work might look something like this:

> Some might say that, in a lot of ways, going to school is similar to having a job. When you go to school, you are expected to be there at a certain time in the morning, and there are consequences for being late. Also, you have to be able to work well with other students and turn in your homework by a certain due date. Just like school, a job also requires that you arrive at a specific time and that you are able to work well with other people. In the same way that homework is due on a certain day, oftentimes a job will require that a project be completed by a given deadline. In these ways, going to school is very much like having a job.

In this version of the passage, notice that all the aspects related to going to school are discussed first and then all the aspects related to having a job are discussed. Instead of a direct, side-by-side comparison of each aspect, the block method tells the reader all about one subject and then all about the other.

So that you can see it more clearly, here's the passage again with everything having to do with going to school underlined and everything related to having a job in italics.

> Some might say that, in a lot of ways, going to school is similar to having a job. [When you go to school, you are expected to be there at a certain time in the morning and there are consequences for being late.] [Also, you have to be able to work well with other students and turn in your homework by a certain due date.] (*Just like school, a job also requires that you arrive at a specific time and that you are able to work well with other people.*) (*In the same way that homework is due on a certain day, often times a job will require that a project be completed by a given deadline.*) In these ways, going to school is very much like having a job.

As you can see, everything related to going to school is discussed first and everything related to having a job is discussed second. The block method is like two blocks, one on top of the other.

INSIDE TRACK

AS YOU'RE READING, try using pens or highlighters of two different colors to highlight, underline, or circle the aspects discussed. Use one color for one subject and another color for the other. This will help you see at a glance which substructure is being used.

INSIDE TRACK

TRY MAKING A chart like this to organize your information.

	Aspect #1	Aspect #2	Aspect #3
Subject A			
Subject B			

PACE YOURSELF

IF YOU WERE to compare two things, which method would you use? Is there one that seems more natural or logical to you?

PRACTICE LAP

Read the passage, and then answer the questions that follow.

In many ways, baking is similar to math. It's true! In math, you use formulas to solve problems, and in baking, you use formulas to create a cake. Both in math and in baking, the formulas involve numbers. In math, you make calculations to solve a problem, and in the same way for baking, the amount of an ingredient needs to be divided or multiplied to make a different size cake. Also, in math class you learn about various shapes and what it means to divide those shapes into halves and quarters as part of a larger understanding of how things fit into space. Baking also involves thinking about how shapes fit into space. Different types of baked goods require different sizes and shapes of pans and are meant to be served by cutting them into various segments of the whole, just like in math!

9. What two subjects are being discussed in the passage?

10. Are the subjects being compared or contrasted?

11. What aspects of each subject are mentioned?

12. Is the passage written in the point-by-point method or the block method?

Check your answers on page 67.

LET'S RECAP

We naturally compare and contrast things every day. We do it so often that we probably don't even realize we're doing it. But we do, and so do authors. They will compare and contrast for two main reasons. One, they might want to highlight information by showing you how it stacks up against something else. Two, they might want to offer you a new perspective. Either way, it's something to look out for in the things you read.

When two or more things are being compared, their similarities are highlighted. When two or more things are being contrasted, their differences are highlighted. So how can you tell whether the author is comparing or contrasting? First, you want to look for the main idea of the passage, which, at this point, you should be getting good at finding. It should tell you whether the subject matter is being compared or contrasted. Just look for the telltale words and phrases.

Remember that there are two different ways an author might compare or contrast something: point-by-point or the block method. Point-by-point occurs when the author talks about each aspect with respect to how it relates to one thing and then how it relates to the other. It's a direct, side-by-side discussion. On the other hand, the block method occurs when the author discusses all aspects of one thing and then moves on to discuss all aspects of the second thing. You'll come across both structures as you read. It's important to be able to distinguish between them so you understand the similarities or differences the author is communicating to you.

ANSWERS

1. compared
   This sentence states that reading is similar to watching a movie. You can tell things are being compared because of the clue word *like*.
2. contrasted
   The word *although* is a clue that snow-skiing and water-skiing are being contrasted.
3. compared
   The sentence has an implied *like*. Laughter is *like* medicine for the sad.
4. compared
   The clue words *in common* signal a comparison.
5. contrasted
   The word *different* is used to refer to running and swimming, which is a clue to the fact that the two are being contrasted.
6. compared
   Dollar coins are being compared to all the other coins. *Similar* is the word that should have clued you in to the comparison.

7. compared

Similar is used in this question to refer to bricks and stones, so we know that they are being compared.

8. contrasted

Because the laptop has advantages that the desktop does not have, it is different. So, the two are being contrasted.

Here is the passage that is referred to in questions 9 through 12.

In many ways, <u>baking</u> is similar to <u>math</u> that you might learn in class. [While in math class you use formulas to solve problems, <u>similarly</u>, in baking you use a formula to create a cake. Both in math and in baking, the formulas involve numbers.] [In math, calculations are needed to solve a problem, and <u>in the same way</u> for baking, the amount of an ingredient needs to be divided or multiplied in order to make a different size cake.] [<u>Also</u>, in math class you learn about various shapes and what it means to divide those shapes into halves and quarters, as part of a larger understanding of how things fit into space. Baking <u>also</u> involves thinking about how shapes fit into space. Different types of baked goods require different sizes and shapes of pans and are meant to be served by cutting them into various segments of the whole, just <u>like</u> in math!]

9. The two subjects being discussed are math and baking.

The two subjects are first mentioned in the topic sentence of the paragraph. They are underlined for you in the passage.

10. The subjects are being compared.

There are some clue words and phrases that should have tipped you off to the fact that math and baking were being compared, as opposed to being contrasted. The words are underlined in the passage and are listed here:

similarly
in the same way
also
like

11. Here are the aspects mentioned: Both use formulas that involve numbers, calculations are needed for both, and both deal with spatial qualities and fractions of a whole.

   As you read the passage, you could've made a chart to help you sort out the different aspects that are being discussed. In the reprint of the passage, the discussion of each aspect has been set aside in brackets.

12. The passage is written in the point-by-point method.

   The point-by-point method is when each aspect is discussed as it relates to both subjects. The other method, block method, discusses each subject fully and then moves on to the next.

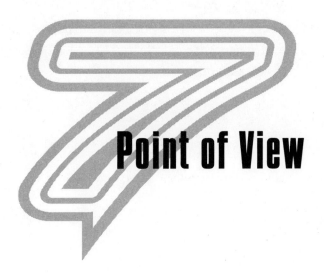

Point of View

Imagine you're standing on the sidewalk of a busy street, holding onto a balloon. Someone bumps into you, causing you to accidentally let go of the balloon. You look up to see it rising against the sky.

Now imagine you're the balloon and someone's holding onto you while standing on the sidewalk of a busy street. Suddenly someone bumps into the person holding you and you feel yourself rising into the sky. You look down at the street as it gets smaller and smaller and you rise higher and higher.

PACE YOURSELF

WRITE A SHORT story from the point of view of your pen or pencil.

This is an example of one scene told from two different points of view. In the first paragraph, the events are told from the perspective of the person holding the balloon. The second paragraph tells the same story, but from the perspective of the balloon itself. That's what **point of view** means. It's the perspective through which all the information is funneled.

Whenever someone writes something that someone else reads, there's a kind of relationship formed between the writer and the reader. Point of view is one of the very first features of a piece of writing that helps to define that relationship. We'll discuss how that happens in a little bit, but first, let's learn about the three different kinds of point of view.

INSIDE TRACK

WHEN YOU THINK about point of view, think about who is talking and who he or she (or even it!) is talking to.

FIRST PERSON

The **first-person point of view** is personal. It's when the writer uses his or her own thoughts and feelings to express the main idea. Literature written in the first person has a narrator who is a character in the story. For example, most people would write a letter using the first-person point of view.

> Dear Aunt Jane,
>
> I am writing to thank you for taking Mark and me to the amusement park this past weekend. We had such a good time riding the roller coasters, the Ferris wheel, and all the other rides. It was so nice of you to drive us there and spend the day with us. We hope you had as much fun as we did.
>
> Love,
> Heather

In this example, Heather has written a thank-you letter to her Aunt Jane. It's personal and makes sense written only in the first person. Note that Heather uses certain words to refer to herself and Mark. Look at the letter, with these words underlined:

> Dear Aunt Jane,
>
> <u>I</u> am writing to thank you for taking Mark and <u>me</u> to the amusement park this past weekend. <u>We</u> had such a good time riding the

*roller coasters, the Ferris wheel, and all the other rides. It was
so nice of you to drive <u>us</u> there and spend the day with <u>us</u>. <u>We</u>
hope you had as much fun as <u>we</u> did.*

*Love,
Heather*

As you can see, Heather uses words such as *I*, *me*, *we*, and *us*. These are some
words to look for when determining if text is written in the first person.
Here's a list of first-person words:

I

me

mine

we

our

us

PACE YOURSELF

WRITE A SHORT poem from the first-person point of view.

SECOND PERSON

When the **second-person point of view** is used, the writer speaks directly
to the reader, calling the reader *you*. For example, the following is from a wel-
come pamphlet for new members of a health club:

As a new member of the health club, there are many programs
and facilities of which you can take advantage. On Saturdays and
Sundays, there are swimming classes in the morning, and on
Monday, Wednesday, and Friday, there are tennis lessons on the
main courts. You can pick up a schedule at the front desk for specific times, and remember—if you come for the swimming

classes, don't forget your swimsuit! There are also yoga classes during the week, and whenever the health club is open, you have use of the weight room, the cardio room, and, weather permitting, the outdoor track.

Did you notice that the writer refers to the reader as *you*? *You* and *your* are two important words to look for when you're trying to decide if text is written from the second-person point of view.

CAUTION!

SOME WRITING MAY have both the words *I* and *you*. Don't get confused. Second-person point of view will never use the word *I*; first person always will.

PACE YOURSELF

TRY TO THINK of three other times when it would make sense to write something in the second person.

THIRD PERSON

Unlike first- and second-person points of view, **third-person point of view** is not a personal perspective. Neither the writer nor the reader seems to be directly involved with what is being said. In literature, the narrator's not a character in the story but is on the outside looking in. Read the following paragraph about squirrels.

Squirrels are part of the rodent family, and although they are common in rural and suburban areas, they can be found in urban regions as well. They spend their days searching for fruit, nuts, and seeds to eat and will bury some of their food so that they can dig it up when food is scarce. Before it buries a nut, a squirrel will rub its scent on it so that it will be able to find it later, even under a blanket of snow. Squirrels have very sharp teeth that are constantly growing, which is why squirrels gnaw on trees and branches. It helps keep their teeth at the right length.

Notice that there's no evidence in the paragraph itself of the existence of an author or a reader. Of course, we know they both exist, but the third-person point of view creates a separation between the topic and the people writing and reading about it. Like the other two points of view, third person has some clue words that can tip you off to its use. Here is the paragraph again with those words underlined:

Squirrels are part of the rodent family, and although <u>they</u> are common in rural and suburban areas, <u>they</u> can be found in urban regions as well. <u>They</u> spend <u>their</u> days searching for fruit, nuts, and seeds to eat and will bury some of <u>their</u> food so that <u>they</u> can dig it up when food is scarce. Before <u>it</u> buries a nut, a squirrel will rub <u>its</u> scent on it so that <u>it</u> will be able to find the food later, even under a blanket of snow. Squirrels have very sharp teeth that are constantly growing, which is why squirrels gnaw on trees and branches. It helps keep <u>their</u> teeth at the right length.

The underlined words all refer to the subject of the passage, squirrels. There's no mention of the author or the reader. Here are the words to look for in the third-person point of view:

> he
> him
> his
> she
> her
> hers
> it
> its
> they
> them
> theirs

PACE YOURSELF

PAY ATTENTION TO how many things you read that are written in the third person. Other than the point of view, do they have anything in common?

PRACTICE LAP

Identify whether *first-*, *second-*, or *third-person point of view* is being used in each of the following sentences.

1. I was strolling along in the park when I saw a bird land on a man's head.

2. He arrived at the meeting about five minutes late.

3. You should always look both ways before crossing the street.

4. The Robinsons are planning a vacation for the summer, but they can't decide where to go.

5. My cereal got really soggy this morning, because it sat too long in the milk before I got a chance to eat it.

6. The Internet has become a tool that is indispensable to most people.

7. Did you get the letter I sent you?

8. Fortunately, she wasn't hurt when she fell while ice-skating the other day.

Check your answers on page 82.

WHEN ARE THEY USED?

Why would a writer use the first-person point of view? Usually because it's the most personal, so it's a good way to immediately connect with the reader. The letter that Heather wrote to her Aunt Jane is a personal letter. When Aunt Jane reads the letter, she'll immediately be able to tell that Heather wrote the letter herself. Let's imagine what Heather's letter to her Aunt would be like if she'd written it in the third person.

Dear Aunt Jane,

Heather is writing to thank you for taking Mark and her to the amusement park this past weekend. They had such a good time riding the roller coasters, the Ferris wheel, and all the other rides. It was so nice of you to drive them there and spend the day with them. They hope you had as much fun as they did.

Love,
Heather

Now doesn't that sound silly? It sounds silly because it's a personal letter and the way it's written in the third person, it sounds very impersonal!

The third person point of view is often used because it's much more objective. The passage about the squirrels would seem much less objective, if you noticed the words *I* or *you* in the writing. Essentially the difference is something like the difference between saying, "I saw a squirrel" and "There is a squirrel." The second statement is more objective, because it doesn't include the person who wrote the sentence.

Because we just talked about how the third-person point of view is the best way to appear objective, let's review what it means to be **objective** as opposed to **subjective**.

objective = unaffected by the thoughts and experiences of the speaker or writer

subjective = based on the thoughts and experiences of the speaker or writer

INSIDE TRACK

IF SOMETHING'S WRITTEN in the first person, it's by definition subjective.

CAUTION!

DON'T ASSUME THAT something is objective just because it's written in the third person.

The passage about the squirrel is objective because it's just facts, unaffected by the thoughts and experiences of the writer. We don't even know who the writer is, and the writer doesn't identify himself or herself in the passage. But

Heather's letter to her aunt is subjective because it's based on Heather's thoughts and experiences and she identifies herself as the writer.

PRACTICE LAP

Identify whether the following statements are *objective* or *subjective*.

9. Marco turned the radio on at a high volume.

10. The radio is too loud.

11. We arrived at the weekly Racquetball Club meeting already out of breath from having run inside to escape the downpour.

12. Some people experience an allergic reaction to jewelry that is made from inexpensive metals.

Check your answers on page 82.

Now maybe you're wondering what happened to the second-person point of view. Don't worry, we haven't forgotten about it. In some situations, the second-person point of view is the most logical choice for a writer. As you saw in the example of the health club pamphlet, the second-person point of view is often used when the writing is directed toward a very specific audience. In the case of the pamphlet, the audience is a new member of the health club. Second-person point of view might also be used when the writer's purpose is to teach the reader how to do something. A recipe might be written in the second person, because it's giving *you* (whoever *you* might be) directions on how to cook something. Or the instructions to a board game are probably written in the second person as well. Whenever the audience is very specific, like a chef or a game player, the second-person point of view might be just the right thing.

A passage written in the second person can help readers make assumptions about the intended audience. Because the writer of a second-person point of view text calls the reader *you*, just ask yourself, "Who's the *you*?"

Let's pretend you didn't know that health club passage was from a health club pamphlet. Do you think you'd be able to tell who the intended audience was? Why? Here's the passage again:

> As a new member of the health club, there are many programs and facilities of which you can take advantage. On Saturdays and Sundays, there are swimming classes in the morning, and on Monday, Wednesday, and Friday, there are tennis lessons on the main courts. You can pick up a schedule at the front desk for specific times, and remember—if you come for the swimming classes, don't forget your swimsuit! There are also yoga classes during the week, and whenever the health club is open, you have use of the weight room, the cardio room, and, weather permitting, the outdoor track.

Of course, in this case, it's pretty easy because the first sentence gives it away! What if that sentence wasn't there? You'd still be able to infer whom the passage is for by using your observations skills. Just ask yourself who'd be attending swimming classes and tennis lessons, using a weight room, cardio room, and track. A member of a health club fits perfectly. From the line about picking up a schedule, you can also infer that the member might be new and isn't yet aware of when classes are held.

 PACE YOURSELF

WRITE A PASSAGE in the third person with a specific audience in mind. Have a friend read it when you're finished. Can your friend guess the intended audience?

PRACTICE LAP

Read the passage and then answer the questions that follow.

> To ensure that we are able to comply with any special requests you might have, we ask that you place your order at least two weeks in advance. As a catering service, we pride ourselves on providing you with the highest quality food at the lowest cost. To make our service even more convenient, we also offer free delivery to any location within a 25-mile radius. If for any reason you are not satisfied with any aspect of our company, please don't hesitate to let us know, and if you have any other questions, please contact us at the phone number listed below. Thank you.

13. Which point of view is used in this passage?

14. Who is the *you* in the passage?

15. How do you know who the *you* is?

Check your answers on page 82.

LET'S RECAP

Point of view is the perspective from which a text is written. Who is writing it? Who is the intended audience? These important questions can be answered when you uncover the writer's point of view.

There are three different points of view. A passage is written in the first person when the writer refers to himself or herself as *I*. It's relatively informal and subjective, and directly expresses the thoughts and experiences of the writer. The second-person point of view is a unique perspective in which the author refers to the reader as *you*. It's often for directions and instructions, and for information written for a specific audience. Discover who the *you* is, and you'll discover the author's intended audience. The third-person point of view is one in which neither the author nor the reader is present within the writing itself. People are referred to as *he, she, them*, or other forms of those words. The third-person point of view is formal, businesslike, and objective.

If writing is objective, it's unaffected by the thoughts and experiences of the author. If writing is subjective, it's based on the thoughts and experiences of the author. To sum it up, first person is subjective and third person is objective.

ANSWERS

1. first person
   This clue word *I* signals the first-person point of view.
2. third person
   The clue word *he* signals the third-person point of view.
3. second person
   The clue word *you* signals that the sentence is written in the second-person point of view.
4. third person
   In this sentence, the people are referred to as *the Robinsons* and *they*, which are clues to the third-person point of view.
5. first person
   The clue words *my* and *I* signal the first-person point of view.
6. third person
   This sentence is just a general, detached statement about the Internet, which signals the third-person point of view.
7. second person
   The second-person point of view talks directly to a certain audience using the word *you*. This sentence is a question addressed to a specific *you*.
8. third person
   Because the person in this sentence is referred to as *she*, you can tell that it is written in the third-person point of view.
9. objective
   This statement is unaffected by the thoughts and feelings of the writer. It is purely something that occurred.
10. subjective
    This statement is affected by the thoughts and feelings of the writer. The writer thinks the radio is too loud.

11. subjective

    This sentence, while not stating an opinion, is still subjective, because it is based on the experience of the Racquetball Club members.

12. objective

    This statement is not based on the thoughts of the writer; it's purely a fact.

13. first person and second person

    The passage is addressing a particular person or group of people, and it uses the word *you*. This signals the second-person point of view. The use of *we* and *our* signals first person.

14. The *you* is a potential customer of a catering company.

15. We know from reading the passage that the person or persons writing the passage are from a catering service. The second sentence starts with *As a catering service. . . .* As we read and observe the content of the rest of the passage, we see that the catering company seems to be explaining some basic aspects of its company to the *you*. Knowing this, we can then ask ourselves, who would a catering company be writing to about some basic aspects of their company and service? The answer is, someone who hasn't used their services before (otherwise, the person would already know the company's information).

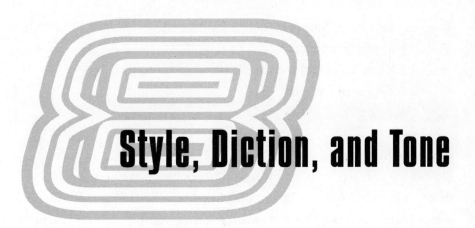

Style, Diction, and Tone

As you've probably already noticed, there's a lot that goes into writing text, and there are a lot of different things for an active reader to observe. Try not to feel overwhelmed by it all. You just want to get as much information as you can from what you read. The more information you get, the better you understand the writer's intentions.

There are three other important features to writing: style, diction, and tone. These are a little more subtle than point of view, but once you know what they are and how to look for them, you'll be further along the road to becoming a successful, active reader.

STYLE

Writers develop **style** to express their ideas. Not everyone enjoys all styles of writing, and style is often a matter of taste. But the style a writer chooses will, like everything else, give you a clue to his or her intentions.

INSIDE TRACK

THINK OF WRITING style as being similar to personal style. We all pick different clothes, have different hairstyles, and wear different accessories as a way of expressing ourselves. Well, style in writing, like sentence structure and descriptions, is the way an author expresses himself or herself.

There are four basic elements of style:

1. sentence structure
2. degree of detail and description
3. degree of formality
4. diction

Sentence Structure

Does the writer use short, simple sentences? Long, complex sentences? Is there a pattern to how the sentences sound to you? Do they all sound the same? Do too many of them start with the same word? Read these two examples. Which has a more pleasing style?

> The man with the beard walked into the room. The man was the basketball coach. The man was there to make sure that the basketball team won their game. The man was going to give the team a pep talk.

> or

> The bearded man was the coach of the basketball team, and he had just walked into the room to give a pep talk to the team. He was going to make sure they won their game.

PACE YOURSELF

WRITE A SERIES of four sentences that all have the same starting word and the same ending word.

Degree of Detail and Description

This element is often explained as the difference between business writing and writing that's intended for pleasure. Ask yourself how specific the author is. How much description does the author use? Read these two examples. Which has the higher degree of detail and description?

Our family lives in a small house on a quiet street. We have a fence around the backyard and big trees in the front.

or

Our family lives in a small blue house with red shutters on the windows. The house is on a quiet street that's lined with mailboxes and cars parked along the concrete curb. We have a long, brown wooden fence around the large backyard and four huge pine trees in the front.

PACE YOURSELF

WRITE TWO DIFFERENT descriptions of the room you're currently in. Make one as descriptive as possible, and make the other simpler.

Degree of Formality
Is the writing casual or formal? Is it friendly, or all business? How does the writer address people? Does he or she say Mr. Jones, or Robert, or Bobby? How much slang, if any, does the writer use? Read these two examples. Which has a higher degree of formality?

Hi Jenny. How are you? I was just wondering if you wanted to go to the movies with me and Myong on Saturday. Let me know when you can. Thanks!

or

Dear Jennifer,
I hope you are well. I am writing to inquire as to whether you would like to join me and Myong for a movie on Saturday. Please respond at your earliest convenience. Thank you.

FUEL FOR THOUGHT

THIS IS THE format for a formal business letter.

[Your name]
[Address]
[Phone number]
[Date]
RE: [What the letter is about]

[Recipient's name]
[Company]
[Address]

Dear [recipient's name]:

[body of letter]

Sincerely,

[your signature]

[your name]

DICTION

What words has the writer chosen? Read these two examples. Why do you think the writer chose those particular words?

Please remove your unwashed feet from the sofa.

or

Get your dirty feet off the couch.

PACE YOURSELF

PAY CLOSE ATTENTION to the words people use when they're talking to you. Think about why they chose the words they did.

Diction means the specific words a writer chooses. As you've probably noticed from looking at a dictionary, there are a lot of words in the English language. So it stands to reason that the decision to choose one word over another must be an important part to writing and must say something about the writer's intentions. A good writer chooses words carefully, making sure they're the best to convey the message of the passage. So, thinking about a writer's diction gives you more information. And, as we've been saying, more information is always good!

FUEL FOR THOUGHT

THE WORD *DICTION* comes from the Latin word *dictio*, which means speaking.

Read the following sentences.

Sentence A: The school's recycling policy has been implemented.

Sentence B: The school's recycling policy has finally been implemented.

You may have noticed that only one word is different between sentence A and sentence B. Sentence B has the word *finally*. Both sentences give the reader the same basic information: The school's recycling policy has been implemented. But by adding the word *finally*, the writer has given us even more information by picking that specific word to make sure the message gets across. What do you think we can infer from the author's use of *finally* in sentence B? Well, it seems to imply that there was some amount of time between the day the policy was first proposed and the day it was implemented. We also get a feeling that the writer has been frustrated waiting for the plan to go into effect. The recycling policy hasn't just been implemented—it's *finally* been implemented. See how just one word can convey another level of meaning within a passage?

Denotation and Connotation

Sometimes words mean exactly what they say, but other times, a different meaning is suggested. It's the difference between denotation and connotation.

> *denotation* = exact meaning

> *connotation* = implied or suggested meaning

INSIDE TRACK

A WORD'S CONNOTATION comes from the context in which it's written, so pay attention to the words around it.

PACE YOURSELF

NOTICE WHAT PEOPLE around you are saying. Do they mean *exactly* what they say? Or is there a connotation?

For example, read the following sentences and notice the difference between them.

> Sentence A: I had a long wait before I saw the doctor.

> Sentence B: I had a protracted wait before I saw the doctor.

You probably noticed that sentence A uses the word *long*, while sentence B uses the word *protracted*. These two words mean essentially the same thing, a large amount of time. But the word *protracted* has a different connotation. When the author chose to use *protracted*, he or she implied the wait was not just long, it was longer than it should have been because there was some sort of delay. As you can see, observing not just the denotation of words, but also the connotation can help you to understand what you're reading.

PRACTICE LAP

What is the connotation of the underlined word in each sentence? Make your best guess based on the context of each word.

1. I was <u>astonished</u> at how good the dinner was.

2. The <u>lax</u> work environment seemed to be hindering productivity.

3. Our annual <u>escape</u> to the cabin by the lake is only one month away.

4. It was <u>gratifying</u> to see Hector finally learn his piano piece.

5. Joanne's <u>pointed</u> comments were sent out in a memo to all the employees.

6. The addition of the fifth speaker in the program was <u>superfluous</u>.

Check your answers on page 96.

TONE

Tone is how a word is said. For example, think about the phrase, *excuse me*. Depending on how you say it, it can mean different things. If you say it like a question, "Excuse me?" it means, "I didn't hear you." If you say it as more of a statement, it can mean, "Can you please move?" It can even mean a sarcastic "I'm sorry," if said with attitude. Try all three and you'll see how important tone can be in determining meaning.

PACE YOURSELF

TRY SAYING THE word *hey* in as many different tones as possible.

Tone applies to writing in much the same way as it does to speech. It can be more difficult, however, to pick up on a writer's tone while you're reading because you don't have the added clues of body language. Don't worry: You might not have body language, but you have context language. The text surrounding a word or phrase can tell you a lot about the tone.

Look at the following two letters.

Letter A:

Dear Client:
Thank you for your letter. We will take your suggestion into consideration. We appreciate your concern.

Letter B:

Dear Valued Customer:
Thank you for your recent letter regarding our refund policy and procedure. We are taking your suggestion quite seriously and truly appreciate your concern.

INSIDE TRACK

UNDERSTANDING THE TONE of the text isn't an exact science, so don't forget to use your instincts.

Notice how different the tone is in the two letters? The tone of letter A is fairly indifferent, while the tone of letter B is sincere and apologetic. What accounts for the difference in tone? Once you're able to identify what it is that gives writing one tone versus another, you'll be well on your way to being a successful reader.

What is it about letter A that makes it seem indifferent—like the person writing it doesn't care much about the client? And what is it about letter B that seems sincere and apologetic? Well, using your observation skills, go over the four elements that make up a passage's style and see if you can identify each element in the letters.

Sentence Structure:
- ➡ Letter A has three relatively short and concise sentences.
- ➡ Letter B has two longer sentences instead of three shorter ones.

Degree of Detail and Description:
- ➡ Letter A lacks detail and description.
- ➡ Letter B describes what the letter was regarding and details how the situation will be handled.

Degree of Formality:
- ➡ Letter A is formal.
- ➡ Letter B is formal, but not as formal as letter A.

Diction:
- ➡ Letter A uses the word *client*.
- ➡ Letter B uses the words *valued customer*.

Now that you've seen the differences in style between the two letters, you see that they have very different tones. But what about the style creates the tone? Letter A's short sentences give it a choppy sound, making it less inviting than letter B's longer, more friendly sentences. Letter B's description gives a sense that the writer has taken time to think about the letter and the problem. Again, letter A is much more formal and detached from the situation. Lastly, letter B calls the reader a *valued customer* instead of just a *client*. This shows some level of caring on the part of the letter's author.

As you can see, there isn't just one thing that determines the tone. Many things decide how the reader feels about what's being said and what the author hopes to communicate. The types of sentences used, the diction, and how something is said, all contribute to the tone in writing.

Just as in speech, there are many tones a writer could use. Here are a few words that might describe a writer's tone:

cheerful	sarcastic
complimentary	ironic
hopeful	wistful
sad	foreboding
gloomy	playful
apologetic	sincere
critical	insincere
insecure	authoritative
disrespectful	threatening
humorous	indifferent

INSIDE TRACK

A PIECE OF writing can have more than one tone.

PACE YOURSELF

PICK A TONE from the list and write a paragraph using that tone. Read it over when you're finished. Notice the words you used and how you structured your sentences.

PRACTICE LAP

Identify the tone of each sentence by choosing a word from the list on page 94.

7. I really didn't mean to scare you like that.

8. The dog stood all alone in the middle of the empty field.

9. It doesn't matter what you say, only what you do.

10. I walked along, kicking a stone down the path in front of me.

11. If you ever want to come here again, then keep off the grass.

12. Just because you're my teacher doesn't mean I have to listen to you.

13. It seems to be a problem.

14. Someday the mail will arrive on time.

15. Hey, Tommy, watch this!

Check your answers on page 96.

LET'S RECAP

Style, diction, and tone are all elements of writing that are a little more subtle than elements like structure and point of view. Style is a combination of sentence structure, degree of detail and description, degree of formality, and diction. Are the sentences long or short? Is there a lot of detail or almost none? Is the writing formal or informal? What words has the author carefully chosen? These are examples of questions to ask yourself when considering the style of a passage.

Diction refers to an author's choice of words. Some words, when used in certain contexts, have certain connotations, or implied meanings. Denotation is the exact meaning of the word. So be sure to notice how an author uses words. It's important for your ability to understand what the author is trying to tell you.

Tone is how something is said. There are many different ways to say the same thing. When you read something, notice its tone. Is it humorous or sincere? Is it angry or apologetic? Is it thoughtful or indifferent? You get the idea.

ANSWERS

1. *Astonished* means surprised, but the connotation is that dinner is not usually good.
2. *Lax* implies that someone was sloppy or careless.
3. *Escape* implies not only going on vacation, but also trying to leave something behind.
4. The fact that the author is *gratified* implies that he or she feels some responsibility for the feat.
5. The connotation is that Joanne's comments were not only sharp and critical, but unnecessary.
6. *Superfluous* implies not only an extra speaker, but also that the addition of the fifth speaker was a waste of time.

The answers to the following questions may have more than one correct answer. Tone is something that can sometimes be interpreted in more than one way. Your answers should resemble these.

7. apologetic

You see from the content that it's an apology, and the tone is sincere.
8. sad

The dog being *all alone* in an *empty* field gives a sad tone
9. sincere

This is direct, to the point, and not sarcastic.
10. wistful

This has a wistful tone, because kicking a stone down a path is a contemplative scene.
11. threatening

This is a threat.
12. disrespectful

This is a disrespectful thing to say to a teacher.
13. indifferent

The person doesn't seem to care about the problem.
14. hopeful

This expresses a hope that one day the mail will arrive on time.
15. playful

The exclamation mark and calling the person Tommy, denotes an informal, playful tone.

Emotional versus Logical Appeal

When a person wants to convince you of something, he or she is probably going to pull out all the stops. Writers use every technique they can think of to win you over to their side of an issue. You've undoubtedly been in situations where someone was trying to convince you of something; you're bombarded with TV and print ads all day that try to persuade you to do something, buy something, or think a certain way. As the attempt to convince you is going on, you were probably searching the argument for reasons. Why should you agree or see this other person's point of view? To be convinced, you need a reason, and the reason has to have enough substance or clout to really convince you.

PACE YOURSELF

TRY CONVINCING FRIENDS or family of something without giving them any reasons. Are they convinced? Or, think about the last time friends or family members tried to convince you of something. What did they use as their reasons?

Imagine you have a friend who plans to try out for the track team at your school and wants you to try out, too. Let's say you're not too sure about whether you should try out, so your friend tries to convince you. What are some reasons your friend might use to persuade you? Imagine that this is your friend's list of reasons:

Reason #1: It will be fun.

Reason #2: They say exercise is good for you, and running track is good exercise.

Reason #3: You're a good runner and will probably make the team.

Reason #4: You'll get to travel to other schools, getting a chance to see other places and people you might not otherwise see.

Reason #5: If you don't try out, you'll just be lazy.

Your friend uses two different kinds of arguments, or reasons. Writers do that too. In an attempt to persuade you, a writer, or anyone else, may use an emotional appeal, a logical appeal, or a combination of both. Here's the difference between the two:

emotional appeal = plays on your emotions or feelings

logical appeal = states actual facts

FUEL FOR THOUGHT

AN *APPEAL* IS an earnest plea.

Now that you know the two types of appeals, let's go back to the argument your friend was making and talk about the reasons. Here was the first reason:

It will be fun.

Does this seem like an emotional appeal or a logical appeal? It seems to appeal to emotion more than reasons, because your friend provides no evidence of how running track will be fun. What will make it fun? But you probably do want to have fun, so this reason appeals to your emotions.

Let's review the second reason your friend gave:

> They say that exercise is good for you, and running track is good exercise.

This reason doesn't play to your emotions. It just logically states a fact. It can be proven that exercise is good for you, and running is exercise. So, running on the track team would be good for you. Now, that's a logical appeal!

What about the fourth reason?

> You'll get to travel to other schools, getting a chance to see other places and people you might not otherwise see.

Well, because the team does travel to other schools, this is another logical reason why you should try out for the team!

What do you think about the last reason that your friend gave? Do you think it's an emotional appeal or a logical appeal?

> If you don't join, you'll just be lazy.

If you think it's an emotional appeal, you're right! Basically, your friend is calling you lazy for not going to the tryouts. It's almost a threat. Don't join and everyone will know you're lazy! This is meant to get you riled up, to incite feelings in you that will be strong enough to make you go to the tryouts!

You can see why it's important to know when someone is trying to convince you by appealing to your emotions, rather than your mind. The person who appeals to your emotions may be hoping you'll go with that emotion and throw your sense of reason out the window. But whenever you're deciding between two or more sides of an argument, it's always best to keep your sense of reason on the alert.

To review the difference between the two types of appeals, take a look at these arguments in favor of an increased amount of physical education time in schools.

Argument #1: There should be more time set aside for physical education in schools. Exercise is important to every student's health, and we wouldn't want students to become lazy and gain weight, which would lead to other health problems. Also, children need time to relax and release stress, so that they can be happy and do better in school.

Argument #2: There should be more time set aside for physical education in schools. Studies show that children who exercise on a regular basis are better able to maintain a healthy weight and have fewer overall health problems than children who don't get enough exercise. Also, there is data to support that regular exercise actually acts as a stress reliever, and students who exercise have been shown to be happy and achieve higher test scores.

The first thing to do when confronted with an argument is to think about the reasons given to justify a position. What reasons does the author of argument #1 give?

Reason #1: Exercise is important to students' health.

Reason #2: Students who don't exercise become lazy and gain weight.

Reason #3: Students who exercise are happier and do better in school.

INSIDE TRACK

IT MIGHT HELP if you go back to the passage and highlight, underline, or circle the author's reasons or number them as you go. Don't be afraid to mark up your paper!

Are these reasons logical or do they appeal only to your emotions? On the surface, they may all seem like good reasons. We probably all want students to be healthy, motivated, and happy. We probably all want students to do better in school. But what evidence does this author give for how more exercise will help? None. Instead, the author appeals to the emotions by trying to convince you based on the fact that you care about the kids!

Reread argument #2:

> There should be more time set aside for physical education in schools. Studies show that children who exercise on a regular basis are better able to maintain a healthy weight and have fewer overall health problems than children who don't get enough exercise. Also, there is data to support that regular exercise actually acts as a stress reliever, and students who exercise have been shown to be happy and acheve higher test scores.

Do you see how it's different? The author basically gives the same reasons, but instead of appealing to your emotions, he or she appeals to your sense of logic. The author tells you there's data to support what he or she is saying. So, instead of just feeling bad for the kids, you can think logically about whether more exercise will be beneficial to them or not.

When faced with an argument in writing, follow these steps:

> Step #1: Identify the issue.
>
> Step #2: Identify the position the author has taken.
>
> Step #3: Identify the reasons the author gives as support for that position.
>
> Step #4: Decide if the reasons are logical or only appeal to your emotions.

An emotional appeal can add strength to a logical argument, but an argument that is *only* emotional is something to watch out for. Such arguments may not have any logical basis at all, and you could be sucked in by words that are only meant to make you feel a certain way, and not think. That's how people get caught up in scams! In reading and in life, you want to be able to make an informed decision when someone tries to persuade you to give money, to buy something, to volunteer to do something, or to give your vote to a particular presidential candidate!

CAUTION!

WHEN THINKING ABOUT the strength of an argument, try to be objective. If you feel a strong emotional pull toward one side of an argument, it could cloud your ability to determine whether the author is being logical or using just emotional appeal.

PACE YOURSELF

THINK OF SOMETHING you'd like to persuade someone to do or believe. Identify three reasons you'd use in your argument, and decide if they're logical or emotional appeals.

PRACTICE LAP

Decide whether each argument is an *emotional* or a *logical* appeal.

1. Public parks should be closed at night, because they're dangerous for people to walk through in the dark.

2. Using cell phones while driving has been shown to cause accidents and therefore should be banned.

3. Data suggests there is a correlation between test scores and the amount of sleep a student gets the night before. So, it's important to get a good night's sleep before a test.

4. It's important to cook with your kids because it makes them happy.

5. Adopt a pet. Studies have shown that people who have pets have lower blood pressure than people without pets.

6. Art classes should be kept in the school's curriculum because creativity is essential to maintaining students' imaginations.

7. Studies have shown that doing crossword puzzles on a regular basis can keep your mind sharp well into old age.

8. Making pizza at home instead of ordering out is more fun and saves money too!

9. Ice-skating is not only a fun winter activity, but it's also good for practicing your balance.

10. In crash tests, cars that have side-impact airbags have a much lower rate of injury than cars that don't have them.

Check your answers on page 104.

LET'S RECAP

Sometimes authors try to persuade their readers to do something or think a particular way. To do this, the authors appeal to either the readers' emotions, their sense of reason, or a little bit of each. An emotional appeal is one that relates to feelings, and a logical appeal is one that relates to the mind and reason.

Beware of arguments that are purely emotional. An author may try to persuade you by making you feel a certain way, instead of relying on your intelligence. Logical arguments are always stronger. Remember what you learned about facts and opinions? Well, facts are logical things we know are true, and when used to support an argument, facts make it stronger.

This chapter was important because when you approach writing, it's good to be armed with as much information as possible. If you can dissect an author's argument and identify when he or she is only appealing to your emotions and is not backing up a specific argument with facts, you'll be better prepared to make decisions about what you read.

ANSWERS

1. emotional

   This is an emotional appeal, because it does not offer any sort of data regarding the dangerousness of the park at night. The argument is meant to appeal to the reader's fears.

2. logical

   This is a logical appeal because it offers evidence of cell phone use causing an increase in accidents.

3. logical

   Again, this is a logical appeal because it isn't just trying to relate to the reader's emotions. It offers evidence that there is a correlation between test scores and the amount of sleep that students receive.

4. emotional

   There is no evidence that cooking makes kids happy. It is purely meant to appeal to readers' sense of caring for their kids.

5. logical

   Because this appeal cites studies that prove people with pets have lower blood pressure, it is a logical appeal.

6. emotional

   The reader of this appeal probably cares about kids and likes the idea of maintaining kids' imaginations, but there's no evidence to suggest creativity is essential to the process.

7. logical

   In this appeal, the author refers to studies that show crossword puzzles are helpful in keeping your mind sharp. The mention of these studies shows that the author wants to appeal to the reader's sense of reason. So, this is a logical appeal.

8. emotional

   There is no proof that making pizza at home is more fun or that it saves money. But, because saving money and having fun are things that many people like to do, the author is appealing to the reader's emotions.

9. emotional

   From this appeal, we don't really know for sure that ice-skating is good for your balance, so it doesn't appeal to reason. It is an emotional appeal.

10. logical

    Crash tests results are mentioned in this argument to appeal to the reader's sense of reason. So, this is a logical appeal.

Meaning in Literature

When it comes to literature, the features of writing that we've been talking about may seem a lot less obvious. It's much more common to read a poem, short story, novel, or play and think to yourself, "I don't get it!" Well, "getting it" is definitely what you want to do. Things might not be as obvious as in nonfiction, but those same features are there in fiction, or literature. And we're going to discover how to identify them!

Just for a minute, let's review stuff we know you know, like the difference between fiction and nonfiction. Fiction is writing short stories, novels, plays, and poems. Nonfiction is newspapers, magazines, encyclopedias, textbooks, and cookbooks. Sometimes there may be fiction, like a poem or short story, in a nonfiction magazine, so it helps to know some characteristics of each:

Fiction	Nonfiction
has at least one character	may or may not have characters
characters are usually not real, and may not even be be human	if there are any characters, they are—or were at one time—real live people
has a plot, or series of events that take place	may or may not involve a story line
may be about real or imaginary places, things, and events	always about real places, real things, and real events

PACE YOURSELF

FIND A POEM you once read but didn't understand. After reading this chapter, reread the poem. See if you can find its theme. Then, identify its subject.

MAIN IDEA VERSUS THEME

In literature, there's a main idea, but it isn't called a main idea, it's called the **theme**. Just like the main idea in nonfiction is different from the subject, the theme in fiction is different from the subject. The subject of a poem might be love, but the theme would be what the author is saying about love.

Literature is often long. Even short stories are usually many pages, so because we don't have that much room in this book, we're going to use poetry as an example of fiction. Poems can be very intimidating. Even more often than novels, poems can illicit that dreaded "I don't get it" from readers. But we're going to be active readers. We're going to dive right in and dissect poetry so you'll know how to do it yourself!

FUEL FOR THOUGHT

A SHORT STORY is usually anywhere between 1,000 and 20,000 words long.

Remember that in the very first chapter of this book we talked about finding out all the basic information? Well, once you extract the basics from a poem, you then can ask, "What does it mean?"

CAUTION!

DON'T LET THE length of a poem intimidate you. Finding the theme is the same whether the poem is one stanza or ten.

FUEL FOR THOUGHT

A STANZA IS a part of a poem made up of a series of lines arranged together, sometimes with a repeating pattern of meter and rhyme. (In other words, it's sort of like a paragraph for poems.)

Let's read the following poem "I Wandered Lonely as a Cloud" by William Wordsworth and first see if we can distinguish its subject from its theme:

> I wandered lonely as a cloud
> That floats on high o'er vales and hills,
> When all at once I saw a crowd,
> A host, of golden daffodils;
> Beside the lake, beneath the trees,
> Fluttering and dancing in the breeze.
>
> Continuous as the stars that shine
> And twinkle on the milky way,
> They stretched in never-ending line
> Along the margin of a bay:
> Ten thousand saw I at a glance,
> Tossing their heads in sprightly dance.
>
> The waves beside them danced; but they
> Out-did the sparkling waves in glee:
> A poet could not but be gay,
> In such a jocund company:
> I gazed—and gazed—but little thought
> What wealth the show to me had brought:

For oft, when on my couch I lie
In vacant or in pensive mood,
They flash upon that inward eye
Which is the bliss of solitude;
And then my heart with pleasure fills,
And dances with the daffodils.

INSIDE TRACK

IF THERE ARE words you don't know in a poem or story, look them up in a dictionary. It'll be easier to understand the writing if you're sure of what the words mean.

The subject of this poem is daffodils. But clearly there's more to it than that. What about the daffodils? What's being said about the daffodils that could be the theme of the poem? The first step is to figure out the action of the poem, then to discover the tone. The action and the tone are going to lead us to the theme. Here's a little equation to help you remember how to find theme:

action + tone = theme

So, first let's figure out what the action of the poem is. The narrator is wandering around (*I wandered lonely as a cloud*) and sees a lot of daffodils (*I saw a crowd, a host, of golden daffodils*). The breeze is blowing (*fluttering and dancing in the breeze*), and the narrator thinks about the flowers later (*when on my couch I lie . . . they flash upon that inward eye*). All that is action in the poem, but we still don't know the theme. We still don't know what it is that Wordsworth is trying to say about those daffodils! Keep in mind what's going on in the poem while we turn our attention to the language.

Always pay close attention to the words a poet uses. The words are a clue to the emotion of the text. And that emotion can, in turn, help you discover the theme.

Look at the poem again. Notice the words Wordsworth uses to refer to the flowers and what they're doing. In the first stanza, he uses the words *fluttering* and *dance*. In the second stanza, he uses *sprightly*, and in the third stanza, *glee* to describe the emotion of the flowers themselves. What do the words have in common? They all express a kind of happiness and joy. The daffodils seem to be acting out of joy. In contrast, Wordsworth describes the narrator in the last stanza as being *in vacant or in pensive mood. Vacant* and *pensive* are not generally associated with happiness, but when the narrator pictures the daffodils dancing in his mind, his heart fills with pleasure.

So, what does this all mean? What theme do the action and the tone equal? The narrator sees this sea of happy flowers dancing, and doesn't think much about it right then, but later pictures it in his mind and is happy. So we could say that the poem's theme is:

> Memories can bring us joy.

> or

> Nature is not fleeting. It brings us joy through memories.

Either theme fits the poem. One isn't more right than the other. That's the thing about literature; it can be interpreted in many ways. Sometimes there is no one right answer. Only in fables—short stories such as Aesop's *The Tortoise and the Hare*—is the theme, or moral, interpreted for you by the author. (The moral of that fable is *slow and steady wins the race*.) It's always important, however, to make sure the theme encompasses the action and tone of the poem.

PACE YOURSELF

WRITE A POEM with the theme "Kindness is contagious."

Let's look at another poem and extract its theme. This one is called "To You" by Walt Whitman.

> Stranger! If you, passing, meet me, and desire to speak to me,
> why should you not speak to me?
> And why should I not speak to you?

Because we know that action + tone = theme, first we need to figure out what the action of the poem is. The narrator asks a stranger two questions. Okay, so now we know the action, but we need to know the tone. Well, some words that Whitman uses (like *desire* and *speak*) seem to indicate some level of formality, because he could have chosen other, less formal words. But the formality seems less important than the fact that the poem is only three lines long, yet manages to ask two questions! What do you notice about the questions? It might help to read "To You" out loud. Here it is again:

> Stranger! If you, passing, meet me, and desire to speak to me,
> why should you not speak to me?
> And why should I not speak to you?

Doesn't it seem that the narrator already has an answer in mind when he asks the questions? He seems to indicate that the stranger should speak to him. He doesn't ask why the stranger would not speak to him, he asks why the stranger shouldn't. Also notice that the stranger doesn't answer the questions in the poem. He or she doesn't need to. The questions are rhetorical, or symbolic, and that's the tone. The tone of the poem is rhetorical.

Okay, so now we know the action and the tone. So, what's the theme? The narrator is asking a stranger in a rhetorical manner why they shouldn't speak to each other if they want to. From this, we can assume that the theme is something like *we should all get along*, or *we're all just people* or *everyone is equal*. Maybe you can think of a different way to phrase it, but the sentiment is the same. The poem is saying that there really isn't any reason why people shouldn't talk to one another. Any differences we may have aren't great enough to keep us apart.

FIGURATIVE LANGUAGE

Often in poems or other works of literature, authors use **figurative language**—words and phrases that mean something other than their literal meanings. For example, in "I Wandered Lonely as a Cloud," Wordsworth says that the daffodils are *tossing their heads*. Well, daffodils don't really have heads, at least not in the human sense. But by saying that the flowers are tossing their heads, the reader imagines a humanlike quality in the daffodils. In this way, Wordsworth uses personification, figurative language that gives human qualities to nonhuman things, like flowers.

You've probably come across a lot of figurative language. Many expressions use figurative language to get a point across without being literal. After all, that's what an expression is, a figure of speech. Think about this expression:

Kill two birds with one stone.

Now we all know this expression doesn't mean to actually go out and use one stone to kill two birds at the same time. It really has nothing to do with killing birds at all. It just means to get two things done at once. For example, if you listen to your voicemail messages while you wash the dishes, you'd be killing two birds with one stone. That's what figurative language is all about, saying one thing to actually mean something else. Here are samples of other figurative language: idiom (*Get off my back!*), euphemism (instead of saying *he died*, saying *he bought the farm*), simile (*She's as busy as a bee!*), and metaphor (*She was a textbook of human emotions!*).

PACE YOURSELF

THINK OF SOME other expressions or figures of speech you know.

FUEL FOR THOUGHT

PERSONIFICATION IS GIVING human qualities to an animal or object. Animated cartoons are built on personification!

PRACTICE LAP

Read the poem "A Man Said to the Universe" by Stephen Crane, and then answer the questions that follow.

A man said to the universe:
"Sir, I exist!"

"However," replied the universe,
"The fact has not created in me
A sense of obligation."

1. What is the action of this poem?

2. What is the tone of this poem?

3. Which words in the poem are clues to the tone?

4. What in the poem is being personified?

5. How would you describe the universe's attitude in the poem?

6. Based on the universe's tone and the content of what it says, what do you
   think is the theme of the poem?

Check your answers on page 113.

LET'S RECAP

Literature may not be as straightforward as nonfiction, but it can be tackled
in similar ways, step by step. In this chapter, we focused on poetry, but the
same techniques can be applied to other types of nonfiction, like short stories, novels, and plays.

In literature, the main idea is called the theme. And how do you find it?
You follow a simple equation: action + tone = theme. So first, find the
action, and then identify the tone. This may be tricky, but just remember to
observe the words the author chooses because they contribute to the feeling, or tone, of the piece. Does the author use figurative language? Is anything personified? These are good questions to ask. Once you know the
action and tone, think about them. The theme will be a general idea that can
be supported by both the action and the tone.

ANSWERS

1. The action of the poem is a conversation between a person and the universe.

2. The tone of the poem is formal.

3. The words *sir* and *fact* and the phrase *sense of obligation* are all clues to the tone of the poem.

    It is very formal to refer to someone as *sir*. This reference, along with the use of words such as *fact* and *sense of obligation* together give you a sense of the tone.

4. The universe is being personified in the poem. Obviously, the universe doesn't generally have conversations with its occupants, but in this poem, the universe speaks. This action gives the universe a humanlike quality.

5. The universe's attitude in the poem is indifferent. While the man in the poem states his case passionately, the universe stays calm. You can tell that the man is passionate about his existence because of the exclamation point at the end of his statement. In contrast, the universe *replies* very matter-of-factly and without emotion.

6. The theme of this poem is that the universe is indifferent to humanity. The action of the poem, plus the tone of the poem, equals the theme of the poem. The action is a conversation between a man and the universe and since the universe is indifferent to the man's declaration that he exists, the theme of the poem is that the universe is indifferent to humanity.

Posttest

Just like the pretest, this posttest has 50 questions. It includes the same types of questions and should take you no longer than two hours to complete. After you finish the posttest and compare your answers with the answer key that follows, you'll see how much you've learned from this book. For any questions you answer incorrectly, refer back to the chapter that discusses that particular topic. Good luck!

Read the passage and then answer questions 1–4.

> Our school marching band will be participating in the statewide competition being held this Saturday at the fairgrounds. The band has been practicing for over a month and has prepared three different choreographed numbers. According to the lead trombonist, the band has a good chance of winning one of the three awards that will be handed out. Each award consists of a check made out to the school's music department and a trophy. We hope that everyone will be able to join the band at the fairgrounds to cheer them on. They need our support!

1. What is happening at the fairgrounds on Saturday?
   a. The annual town carnival begins.
   b. The high school football team is competing against their rivals.
   c. The marching band is playing in a statewide competition.
   d. The talent show is being held.

2. How many numbers did the band prepare?

    a. two

    b. three

    c. four

    d. five

3. Who thinks the band has a good chance of winning an award?

    a. the football coach

    b. the parents of the band members

    c. the town's mayor

    d. the lead trombonist

4. Will awards will be given? If so, what kinds?

Identify whether each of the following is a *subject* or a *main idea*.

5. prescription eyeglasses

6. recipes for baking cake

7. how to play bridge

8. why magnets attract each other

9. gardening is enjoyable

Read the passage and answer questions 10 and 11.

The local health club began an initiative before this November's election to get people to vote yes to a certain question that would be on the ballot. The question asked whether schools should get rid of snack machines, replacing them with healthier alternatives for students. The health club was in favor of the switch. Unfortunately, the president of the health club had an emergency on the day of the election and didn't make it to her polling station before it closed for the day. When the election results came in, the club saw that they were one vote short of getting rid of the snack machines.

10. How could the result of the election have been different?

11. What is the main idea of this passage?
   a. Elections happen in November.
   b. Schools should get rid of snack machines.
   c. Not everyone must be present to vote in an election.
   d. Every vote counts.

12. A topic sentence is never
   a. a general idea.
   b. supported by other ideas in a paragraph.
   c. so specific that it doesn't need support.
   d. at the beginning of a paragraph.

Identify whether each of the statements in questions 13–17 is a fact or an opinion.

13. Gravity pulls us toward the Earth.

14. Hurricanes have at least 75-mile per hour winds.

15. Everyone should see a dentist at least twice a year.

16. Smoothies are a delicious way to get your recommended fruit intake.

17. Stop signs are red.

18. On another sheet of paper, rewrite the following paragraph so that it's in chronological order.

After the chanting died down, our principal gave a short speech about how excited he was for the football game. Then we all chanted our school's motto to the beat of the drums. Finally, the pep rally ended with the marching band playing a couple more songs and marching off the field. This afternoon's pep rally began with the marching band coming out onto the football field and playing our school's fight song. The speech ended with an introduction of the starting seniors on the team.

For questions 19–23, identify in your own words the *cause* and *effect* in each statement.

19. George has a scar on his knee from a cut he got while playing hockey.

20. I covered my mouth because I sneezed.

21. They say that painting a wall blue creates a relaxing mood in a room.

22. The overflowing trash was causing the kitchen to stink.

23. The effect of Harry's hard work was that he got an A on his test.

Read the passage and answer questions 24 and 25.

Dear Jill,

Because you asked me to give you advice about whether or not you should join the softball team this spring, I am writing to tell you what I think. I think you should join the team and there are a few reasons why I think this.

First, I think that softball is good exercise and it's important to be active. You wouldn't want to just come home from school and sit in front of the television all afternoon. That wouldn't be good for your body.

Second, I think softball is fun. I played myself when I was your age and had a blast out there on the field with the other girls. I enjoyed competing and challenging myself to be better.

Most importantly, I think it would be a good opportunity for you to make friends. Some of the girls that I met playing softball are still my good friends today. I hope this helps, and good luck!

Sincerely,
Heather

24. List the reasons Heather gives Jill for why she should play softball in the order that they appear in the letter.

25. What do you notice about the order in which the reasons appear?

Read the passage and answer questions 26 and 27.

Eating ice cream out of a cone is very different than eating it out of a cup. For one thing, when you eat ice cream from a cone, you don't need a spoon. You can just use your mouth as your utensil. You also won't have any trash to throw away when you're done, because you don't use a spoon and you can eat the cone! Eating from a cone is a little bit messier, though, because the ice cream is likely to drip down the side if you don't lick fast enough. Most likely if you eat your ice cream out of cup, you're going to need a spoon. And because you'll then have a spoon and a cup, you'll need to find a trash can when you're done eating. Also, eating ice cream from a cup can be a lot less messy than eating from a cone.

26. Are eating ice cream from a cone and eating it from a cup being compared or contrasted in the passage?

27. What three aspects of ice cream eating are mentioned?

For questions 28–32, identify whether the *first, second,* or *third-person point of view* is being used in each sentence.

28. I heard you the first time.

29. Pocket watches are less popular than they once were.

30. Four years ago was my first year of high school.

31. It's nice to write a thank-you note to someone who has given you a gift.

32. Sally and Linda have been friends for more than 20 years.

Identify whether each sentence in questions 33–37 is *objective* or *subjective*.

33. Yesterday, I got in trouble for having my cell phone on in class.

34. The first automobile was invented around the turn of the century.

35. Learning to ride a bike isn't difficult.

36. Japan is a country in Asia.

37. Franklin Pierce was the fourteenth president of the United States.

38. What is the connotation of the underlined word in the following sentence?
The state's <u>antiquated</u> voting system has caused problems in recent elections.

Identify which word (*authoritative, indifferent, uncertain,* or *critical*) describes the tone of each sentence in questions 39–42.

39. I guess it's raining outside.

40. You really should've studied more for that test.

41. I think that the poem might have something to do with love.

42. This poem is definitely about love.

For questions 43–47, identify whether each sentence is a *logical* or an *emotional* appeal.

43. The Environmental Protection Agency says we need to make sure there isn't any mold in our schools because it's unhealthy for the students and teachers. Exposure to mold can cause allergies and illness.

44. Photography is a good hobby for those who would like to feel more connected to their surroundings.

45. There is data that points to a connection between eating apples and increased memory.

46. Studies have shown that more public park space in a community actually decreases the stress of members of that community.

47. Swimming on a daily basis is good for your endurance.

Read the poem "Where My Books Go" by William Butler Yeats and answer the questions that follow.

> All the words that I utter,
> And all the words that I write,
> Must spread out their wings untiring,
> And never rest in their flight,
> Till they come where your sad, sad heart is,
> And sing to you in the night,
> Beyond where the waters are moving,
> Storm-darken'd or starry bright.

48. What is the action of the poem?

49. What is the tone of the poem?

50. What is the theme of the poem?

ANSWERS

1. **c.** The marching band is playing in a statewide competition. (Refresh your knowledge of getting the essential information in Chapter 1.)

2. **b.** The band prepared three numbers. (Refresh your knowledge of getting the essential information in Chapter 1.)

3. **d.** The lead trombonist thinks the band has a good chance of winning. (Refresh your knowledge of getting the essential information in Chapter 1.)

4. Each award consists of a check and a trophy. (Refresh your knowledge of getting the essential information in Chapter 1.)

5. subject

    Prescription eyeglasses are specific objects and therefore do not need support. (To revisit subject versus main idea, look at Chapter 2.)

6. main idea

    This is a main idea because essentially, it has the same meaning as how to bake a cake. In this case, the subject is baking a cake, but what is being *said about* baking a cake? What is being said is how to bake it. (To revisit subject versus main idea, look at Chapter 2.)

7. main idea

    This is a main idea because the subject is the game of bridge, and how to play the game. The *what* and the *how* are being stated. (To revisit subject versus main idea, look at Chapter 2.)

8. main idea

    Why magnets attract each other is a main idea rather than a simple subject because it is a general idea that relies on other ideas for support. (To revisit subject versus main idea, look at Chapter 2.)

9. main idea

    This needs support. Why is gardening enjoyable? The subject is gardening, but the fact that it is enjoyable is what is being *said about* gardening. (To revisit subject versus main idea, look at Chapter 2.)

10. The result could have been different if the president of the club had voted. In the passage, we read that the health club was only one vote short of getting the snack machines in schools switched to healthier alternatives. They were only one vote short, and we assume that if the president had voted, he or she would've voted in favor of the switch and the election would have turned out differently. (To revisit main idea, look at Chapter 2.)

11. **d.** The main idea of the passage is that every vote counts. (To revisit main idea, look at Chapter 2.)

12. **c.** A topic sentence is always a general idea supported by other ideas within the paragraph. It is also usually at the beginning of a paragraph. (To revisit topic sentences, look at Chapter 2.)

13. fact

    It can be proven that gravity pulls us toward the Earth. So, it is a fact. (Refresh your knowledge of fact versus opinion by rereading Chapter 3.)

14. fact

    It can be proven that hurricanes have at least 75-mile per hour winds. Because this cannot be debated, it is a fact. (Refresh your knowledge of fact versus opinion by rereading Chapter 3.)

15. opinion

    Although it seems logical to go to the dentist at least twice a year, it is still something that could be debated. It is possible that someone will disagree. (Refresh your knowledge of fact versus opinion by rereading Chapter 3.)

16. opinion

    Not everyone likes smoothies, so liking them is an opinion. (Refresh your knowledge of fact versus opinion by rereading Chapter 3.)

17. fact

    The color of stop signs is not up for debate. They are red, and this is a fact. (Refresh your knowledge of fact versus opinion by rereading Chapter 3.)

18. *This afternoon's pep rally began with the marching band coming out onto the football field and playing our school's fight song. Then we all chanted our school's motto to the beat of the drums. After the chanting died down, our principal gave a short speech about how excited he was for the football game. The speech ended with an introduction of the starting seniors on the team. Finally, the pep rally ended with the marching band playing a couple more songs and marching off the field.*

    The pep rally beginning clearly comes first, because the whole passage is about what happened at the pep rally. For the same reason, the pep rally ending must come last. Words like *then* clue you in to the order of the rest. *After the chanting died down . . .* must have happened after the chanting began, and you know that the speech had to start before it ended. (Revisit chronological order in Chapter 4.)

19. cause = a cut when playing hockey

    effect = George's scar

    (Revisit cause and effect in Chapter 4.)

20. cause = I sneezed

effect = I covered my mouth

(Revisit cause and effect in Chapter 4.)

21. cause = painting a wall blue

effect = a relaxing mood in the room

(Revisit cause and effect in Chapter 4.)

22. cause = the overflowing trash

effect = the kitchen stinks

(Revisit cause and effect in Chapter 4.)

23. cause = Harry's hard work

effect = an A on his test

(Revisit cause and effect in Chapter 4.)

24. The reasons are softball is good exercise, softball is fun, and playing softball is a good opportunity to make friends. (Revisit order of importance in Chapter 5.)

25. The reasons appear in order or importance, starting with the least important and ending with the most important. (Revisit order of importance in Chapter 5.)

Here is the passage that pertains to questions 26 and 27 with the relevant information underlined.

Eating ice cream out of a cone is very <u>different</u> than eating it out of a cup. For one thing, when you eat ice cream from a cone, <u>you don't need a spoon</u>. You can just use your mouth as your utensil. You also <u>won't have any trash to throw away</u> when you're done, because you don't use a spoon and you can eat the cone! <u>Eating from a cone is a little bit messier,</u> though, because the ice cream is likely to drip down the side if you don't lick fast enough. Most likely if you eat your ice cream out of cup, <u>you're going to need a spoon</u>. And because you'll then have a spoon and a cup, <u>you'll need to find a trash can</u>, when you're done eating. Also, <u>eating ice cream from a cup can be a lot less messy</u> than eating from a cone.

26. Eating ice cream from a cone is being contrasted with eating ice cream from a cup.

The very first sentence indicates that the two are being contrasted, because it states that they are *different*. (To revisit compare and contrast, look at Chapter 6.)

27. The three aspects mentioned are to need or not to need a spoon, having or not having trash, and the messiness of eating.

You can find all of these aspects by reading the passage carefully. Notice that in this passage, all three aspects as they relate to eating from a cone are discussed first and then all three aspects as they relate to eating from a cup are discussed second. This is a block method contrast. (To revisit compare and contrast, look at Chapter 6.)

28. first person

Don't let the *you* in this sentence throw you off. The author is identified as *I*, which makes this the first-person point of view. (Refresh your knowledge of point of view in Chapter 7.)

29. third person

This is merely a statement made about pocket watches. There is no evidence of either the author or reader. (Refresh your knowledge of point of view in Chapter 7.)

30. first person

The use of the word *my* signals the first person. (Refresh your knowledge of point of view in Chapter 7.)

31. second person

A thank-you note is an object, so the *you* here is not a clue. But the *you* at the end of the sentence refers to the reader, so this sentence is written in the second-person point of view. (Refresh your knowledge of point of view in Chapter 7.)

32. third person

Neither Sally, Linda, nor the reader is present in this sentence, so it is written in the third-person point of view. (Refresh your knowledge of point of view in Chapter 7.)

33. subjective

Getting in trouble for having *my* cell phone on in class is something experienced. The word *my* is a clue that is one person's specific experience, so the statement is subjective. (Refresh your knowledge of subjective in Chapter 7.)

34. objective

This is an objective statement about when cars were invented. It has nothing to do with the author's experience. (Refresh your knowledge of objective in Chapter 7.)

35. subjective

The author of this sentence thinks learning to ride a bike is not difficult, but this is an opinion. It is expressed as it relates to the author's experience and is, therefore, subjective. (Refresh your knowledge of subjective in Chapter 7.)

36. objective

This statement is not influenced by the author's experiences, so it is objective. (Refresh your knowledge of objective in Chapter 7.)

37. objective

The fact that Franklin Pierce was the fourteenth president is not influenced by the author's experiences. It is an objective fact. (Refresh your knowledge of objective in Chapter 7.)

38. The author uses *antiquated* instead of *old* to imply not just that the voting system is old, but that it is so old, it's no longer useful. (To revisit style, look at Chapter 8.)

39. indifferent

The author says *I guess,* which gives a feeling of not caring. (To revisit diction, look at Chapter 8.)

40. critical

This situation warrants a critical tone. The phrase *You really should've* implies there have been or will be unfortunate consequences as a result of not studying more for the test. (To revisit tone, look at Chapter 8.)

41. uncertain

The author is unsure, and you can tell by the use of the words *think* and *might.* (To revisit diction, look at Chapter 8.)

42. authoritative

The author says *definitely* and is very certain the poem is about love. This certainty shows confidence and authority in the subject of poetry. (To revisit tone, look at Chapter 8.)

43. logical

The Environmental Protection Agency (EPA) is a United States govern-
ment agency whose goal is to protect health and the environment. Mentioning the EPA's suggestion to make sure there is no mold because it's
unhealthy strengthens this argument. It is true that mold can cause allergies
and illness, so this is a logical appeal. (Revisit logical appeal in Chapter 9.)

44. emotional

It might be nice to feel more connected to your surroundings, but this
argument offers no evidence that proves photography accomplishes that
connection. (Revisit emotional appeal in Chapter 9.)

45. logical

This is a logical appeal because it creates a situation in which the reader
must use reason to think about the connection between eating apples
and the increase in memory. (Revisit logical appeal in Chapter 9.)

46. logical

The fact that there is a study to show that more park space can decrease
stress appeals to the reader's sense of reason, not his or her emotions.
So, this is a logical appeal. (Revisit logical appeal in Chapter 9.)

47. emotional

Increasing your endurance is a good goal, but this appeal offers no evidence that swimming on a daily basis will help. It does not appeal to the
reader's sense of reason. (Revisit emotional appeal in Chapter 9.)

Here is the poem "Where My Books Go" by William Butler Yeats that pertains to questions 48 through 50. Some words and phrases have been underlined to help explain the answers.

All the words that I utter,
And all the words that I write,
Must spread out their wings untiring,
And never rest in their flight,
Till they come where your sad, sad heart is,
And sing to you in the night,
Beyond where the waters are moving,
Storm-darken'd or starry bright.

48. The narrator talks about his words as birds that must go out and be read or heard by someone to survive so he pleads with them to go forth.

The first two lines are fairly clear. The narrator is talking about the words he says and the words he writes down. The second two lines talks about his words as if they were birds. They *must spread out their wings* and *never rest in their flight*. The next two lines introduce the reader and explain that he or she is sad. The last two lines emphasis that the words must travel far, regardless of the conditions. (Refresh your knowledge of meaning in literature in Chapter 10.)

49. The tone of this poem is pleading and hopeful.

There are some words and phrases in the poem that should've clued you in to the tone. First of all, Yeats uses the word *all* twice in the first two lines, which emphasizes that all the narrator's words must do what he describes. *Must* is also a clue. The narrator saying that his words *must* do this seems to indicate some doubt that they will accomplish the goal. He's pleading with his words, in a sense, telling them that they *must* do this, because it is important to him. He says they must *never rest*. From this you can see that the tone is both pleading and hopeful. (Refresh your knowledge of meaning in literature in Chapter 10.)

50. The theme of this poem is the idea that writers want and need to reach people through their words, and to make a difference in people's lives.

Action and tone come together to create the theme of the poem. We know that the narrator wants his words to reach the reader, who is sad. The words' effect on the reader is the action that is occurring (*spread out their wings, sing to you in the night*). We also know from the tone of the poem that the narrator feels an urgent need for his words to reach these sad people (*must, never rest*). From this, we can see that the theme of the poem is that writers are very hopeful that their words reach their readers on an emotional and helpful level. Writers want to make a difference in people's lives. (Refresh your knowledge of meaning in literature in Chapter 10.)

Glossary

Active reader: A reader who actively connects with what he or she reads.

Block method: One way an author can structure a comparison or contrast.

Cause: What makes something happen.

Chronological order: A structure of writing in which the author presents events in sequence, or the time order in which they happened.

Clue phrase: A group of words that gives a clue to the author's structure or point of view.

Clue word: A word that gives a clue to the author's structure or point of view.

Compare: To look for ways in which things are alike.

Connotation: The suggested or implied meaning of a word.

Contrast: To look for ways in which things are different.

Degree of detail and description: One of the four elements of writing style; the amount of attention to details and description.

Degree of formality: One of the four elements of writing style; how formal the writing is.

Denotation: The exact meaning of a word.

Diction: One of the four elements of writing style; the author's choice of words.

Effect: What happens as a result of something else.

Emotional appeal: An argument that appeals to the reader's emotions.

Fact: Something that can be proven to be true.

Figurative language: Words that do not have their literal meaning.

First person: A point of view in which the narrator is a character in the story.

Implied main idea: A main idea that is not explicitly stated.

Least important ⟶ most important: One way to organize information, starting with the least important idea and ending with the most important.

Literature: A form of writing such as poems, novels, short stories, and plays.

Logical appeal: An argument that appeals to a reader's sense of reason.

Main idea: What a selection is mostly about.

Most important ⟶ least important: One way to organize information, starting with the most important idea and ending with the least important.

Opinion: A belief.

Order of importance: A text structure in which ideas are arranged based on how important they are.

Perspective: The point of view from which something is written.

Point of view: The first-person, second-person, or third-person perspective from which something is written.

Point-by-point method: One way an author can organize comparisons or contrasts.

Second person: A point of view in which the reader is directly referred to as *you*.

Sentence structure: One of the four elements of writing style; the kinds of sentences an author uses.

Style: A way in which an author expresses his or her ideas.

Subject: The topic, or what the text is about.

Theme: The message a piece of literature promotes.

Third person: A point of view in which the narrator is not a character in the story.

Tone: The way something is written, such as seriously, humorously, and so on.

Topic sentence: A sentence that expresses the main idea of a passage and often is the first sentence in a paragraph.

Notes

Notes

Notes

Notes

Notes